DANCING *with* God

The Christian Journey to
Live Supernaturally

Marcia Chang Vogl

Copyright © 2024 by Marcia Chang Vogl
No part of this publication may be reproduced, stored in a retrieval system or transmitted in any way by any means, electronic, mechanical, photocopy, recording or otherwise, without the prior permission of the author except as provided by USA copyright law.

All Scripture quotations, unless otherwise indicated, are taken from the Holy Bible, New International Version®, NIV®. Copyright © 1973, 1978, 1984, 2011 by Biblica, Inc.™ Used by permission of Zondervan. All rights reserved worldwide. www.zondervan.com. The "NIV" and "New International Version" are trademarks registered in the United States Patent and Trademark Office by Biblica, Inc.™

Publisher:
Hidden With Christ Ministries
P.O Box 945
Forest, VA 24551
https://hiddenwithchrist.org

Ebook: 978-1-7-354447-4-1
Paperback: 978-1-7354447-3-4
Hardcover: 978-1-7354447-5-8

Endorsements

Marcia Chang Vogl's book *Dancing With God, The Christian Journey to live Supernaturally*, is not a book to gain "head knowledge." Rather this is a book that leads and guides believers to faith and freedom.

The principles, exercises, and prayers outlined in the book transform believers to receive exponential blessings and an overwhelming feeling of God's love.

I have been fortunate to call Marcia a mentor, a life coach, and a spiritual mother. She has helped me experience the meaning of going from "glory to glory." I pray her book will have a far "reach" in transforming lives as she has mine.

— Dr. Cherylin Lew
Assistant Superintendent
Public School Administrator

As the founder of Bethany Projects and a partner with Hidden with Christ Ministries, Marcia is qualified to help readers navigate spiritual blocks. In her second book,

Dancing With God, The Christian Journey to Live Supernaturally, she brings insights into the Christian journey that have practical applications appropriate for almost any situation. The experiential lessons she shares give practical guidance and advice that can bring supernatural results.

— Martin Wiles,
A Whisper in the Woods: Quiet Escapes in a Noisy World
Managing Editor, *Christian Devotions*
Senior Editor, *Inspire a Fire*

―――

I have known Marcia Vogl as an anointed prophetic intercessor, prayer counselor, teacher, and friend for over 35 years. Her life's work is marked by repentance and forgiveness. She uses practical methods to effectively impart spiritual principles. Her illustrations are memorable for learners at all stages of spiritual maturation. Her knowledge of spiritual authority has helped many gain spiritual freedom.

Gail M. Downey
— Public Educator and Consultant

Foreword

After observing the emotional pain suffered by the abandoned children who have come to live in our Children's Home in East Africa, I can say that I have seen firsthand both the fracturing of the human soul as well as its dramatic restoration. But you don't have to have been thrown by the side of the road in Africa to have experienced trauma that crushed your emotions. In our high tech and fast-paced society, multitudes of people are living with emotional damage and can't seem to find healing and wholeness.

This book provides an incredibly practical and biblically sound path to emotional restoration. The insights you will read will resonate with you and you will find yourself saying, "That is it!" Then if you will follow through with the simple exercises laid out in this manual, you will

Foreword

progress from having an intellectual understanding of your struggle to experiencing the freedom that you have longed for all your life.

What is presented here is not just theory but real-world, hands-on, useful tools that will assist you in walking out of the darkness of emotional bondage into the light of freedom. You can use this book to receive healing to your soul and then be enabled to help others. I have been privileged to watch the fruit of Marcia Chang Vogl's teaching and prayer counseling over the past decade and I can attest to its lasting value. You will be blessed as you embark on this journey and will be able to say with the psalmist, "He restores my soul…" (Psalm 23:3)

Rita L. Langeland
Executive Director/Founder
Hidden With Christ Ministries
Treasures of Africa Children's

Contents

INTRODUCTION	1
PROLOGUE	9
JUNKYARD TREASURE	13
THE GREAT EXCHANGE, THE STORY OF SALVATION	17
1. RESCUED FROM EDEN'S EXILE	25
Break the Ball-and-Chain Existence	25
A Second Chance to Succeed	28
The Great Release	37
2. BE STRONG AND TAKE HEART	47
It's An Inside Job	60
Leave the Old, Welcome the New	67
3. BLESSINGS FOR A THOUSAND GENERATIONS	85
Mom and Dad: the First Line of Action	86
Don't Let History Repeat	95
Impact of Infirmity	104
Trails of Iniquity (Isaiah 59: 2)	109
4. IS SIN CROUCHING AT YOUR DOOR? (GENESIS 5:7)	113
Keep the Doors Shut	113
Watch Out for Air Attacks	137
5. LEAVE MISTAKES BEHIND	141
Ask, Seek, and Knock	142
The Call	147
Three Realms	149
Your Alert System	152

6. PREPARING FOR YOUR FUTURE	157
A Suitable Habitation	157
A Worthy Vessel	158
Quality Lifestyle	159
Habitation	162
Financial Order	162
Emotional Order	165
Healthy Relationships	166
The Church Home	168
7. COME CELEBRATE	173
Begin to Dance	176
Amen and Amen	181
Index	183
Also by Marcia Chang Vogl	189

Introduction

When going on any journey, knowing *why* you are on the way is just as important as knowing *where* you are going. The event of accepting Jesus into your life is just the first step of an exciting journey. Before leaping into this book, *Dancing With God, The Christian Journey to Live Supernaturally*, it would be best to understand the premise for calling these "dance steps". This introduction sets the basis of why this journey is important to you, a Christian seeking an intimate relationship with God.

If you suffer or have suffered from emotional and spiritual setbacks, your life will never be "back to normal." This book will show you how your life will be supernaturally better than your past "normal" as you journey forward to dance with God.

Why Am I Here? My Realization Story

As I walked out of the bathroom, a very large woman growled at me. "You are the reason I'm here."

I was a patient in a psychiatric ward at a local hospital where I was admitted for depression. I had been there for only a day, as the only patient assigned to a room with four beds. I chose the bed farthest from the hall door in the corner near a window.

During the afternoon a "Brunhilde" of a woman was admitted and assigned to the bed near the bathroom. Her husband was seated next to her so I quietly slipped past them when I went into the bathroom. It was upon my exit that she startled me.

She said, "You're the reason I'm here. You're supposed to pray for me." I, only 4'10", weighing 98 pounds was intimidated so I was willing to comply with such a demand. At that time, I was not experienced in impromptu praying. I had only prayed using books, devotionals, and other repetitive prayers. I took her hands and prayed something. It probably was a combination of safety for travel, a birthday prayer, and healing. All I knew was to say "Amen" and head for the safety of my bed in the corner.

Introduction

Upon rising the next morning, the woman was gone. I was there for depression where I could not think straight nor carry on a normal life as a wife and mother of three. I followed the hospital life routine of meals, therapy, and naps.

Later in the afternoon, "Brunhilde" came bounding down the hall.

"I've been looking for you! Thank you so much for the prayer. I had the best sleep last night, ever!" she said. "I'm going home today."

"What was that lady here for?" I asked another patient who was in group therapy with her.

"She came in last night for a suicide attempt." Only then did I learn this. She was now happy.

During the next three weeks, I met another patient caught in a dilemma. She was a pregnant unwed mother. Her family would disown her if she birthed the baby and the church would excommunicate her if she had an abortion. She decided suicide was the way out. She was admitted as a suicide patient. In group therapy, I heard from people who heard voices, a woman who tried to kill her infant, and someone who could not stay sober. My problem was minuscule next to these.

I was released after three weeks and started the 2-year journey to recovery from depression and to resume a normal life. But, life after such experiences is never back to normal. I realized the Lord called me to minister to his hurting people. I embarked on years of training, education, and experience to bring inner healing and deliverance to broken people.

Spiritual growth, invisible to the naked eye, is played out in our behaviors, language, and goals. It involves all of your mind, belief system, soul, behaviors, and emotions. Besetting sin, bad habits, and generational sin hinder spiritual growth. These issues are rarely addressed from the pulpit yet Christians are affected daily. Christian counselors include prayer in their sessions but unless the cross of Christ is applied in repentance and forgiveness, there is no significant breakthrough. These following important questions frequently pop up with Christians:

1. How do I move on from the past without old baggage or brokenness?
2. Where is the joy I'm supposed to have?
3. How does my environment impact my spiritual walk?
4. What effect does my family tree have in my spiritual life?
5. How do I avoid making the same mistakes?

Introduction

6. What does it mean to "dance with God" and how do I do that?

Although not in conflict with traditional counseling, you will move closer to the cross of Jesus Christ who is the source of all healing and freedom. These practical applications of repentance and forgiveness will allow you to experience freedom in Christ for yourself.

After many hours of private sessions listening to people's pain and ministering to groups in spiritual workshops, I found that leading them through repentance and forgiveness was the most supernaturally powerful deliverance any of them had ever experienced. The burden of unresolved past life events can be removed. I offer you a journey through a series of simple exercises that help you untangle spiritual conflicts. You will learn "how" you got trapped and how to get out, but not necessarily "why." Only God holds the answers to "why." I will offer key topics you never considered or didn't want to consider. Be ready to write and pray. When you write the answers to the questions, it will clarify your thinking and even identify emotions you were unaware were active. Pray aloud the prayers offered so that you *hear* the power of repentance and forgiveness. Follow all the steps whether you are working individually or in a small group.

Chapter 1, Rescued from Eden's Exile, will give you a working system to tap into the power of repentance and forgiveness. These are the supernatural keys Christians must know have to unlock any chokeholds of sin.

Chapter 2, Be Strong and Take Heart, will restore you to wholeness and joy. God is interested in restoring broken hearts. You do not have to go through life spiritually crippled. You can be healed. "The joy of the Lord is your strength." (Nehemiah 8:10) When your joy is restored and activated you can stand strong in the currents of life.

Chapter 3, Blessings For a Thousand Generations will give you access to the blessings of your family line. Medical and psychological sciences agree that inherited genes and family lifestyle influence your future. Good ones include longevity genes or musical talent, while others are detrimental, like infirmity or emotional dysfunction. Because God is always in the "now," He can touch your past, present, and future all at once. That's supernatural! The exercises and prayers will allow you to disconnect from generational dysfunctions and connect to your generational blessings.

Chapter 4, Is Sin Crouching at your Door? will alert you to five major entrapments: 1.) Innocent Bloodshed, 2.) Sexual Sin, 3.) Covenant breaking, 4.) Idolatry, and 5.) Deception. When you identify how these subtly weave in your life,

Introduction

you can truly disconnect from them and their consequences.

Chapter 5, Leaving Mistakes Behind is a roadmap for making good life choices in the natural and the spiritual realm to live fully blessed in the image of God (Genesis 1:27-28). God wants to supernaturally lavish his love on you, not take from you.

Chapters 6, Preparing for Your Future and Chapter 7, Come Celebrate, point to worship as the doorway to an intimate relationship with God. These final chapters set the stage for you to become God's eternal dance partner through worship.

When you've finished this book, you will learn the practices that will guide you to live supernaturally from glory to glory. The exercises here will allow you to:

- Develop experiences of body, mind, and spirit
- Build a working process that can be adapted to any situation
- Remove roadblocks from your path, thereby eliminating apologies and self-abasement

I became a Christian at age 13. Through the years, I have experienced God in various ways and have learned how to dance with Him. Through my journey and that as a prayer counselor, I developed workshops and taught small groups in my home. My first book, **The Path Forward**, grew out of that experience as we all grew in knowing our Lord and Savior.

Now, as an ordained minister, with a Master and a Doctorate of Practical Ministry degrees from Wagner University, I am the founder and director of Bethany Projects, in partnership with Hidden with Christ Ministries. I specialize in women's ministry and deliverance with a passion for inner healing guiding readers through spiritual blocks with targeted prayer.

I love reaching out to instill life values to others as I have traveled internationally serving as a Global Volunteer in Xian, China, and Hanoi, Vietnam. This book is backed by 30 years of prayer ministry, 49 years of marriage, and experience as a full- time mom raising an international family of three children, two of whom are adopted.

Prologue

The "forgiveness of sin" kept nagging at me. I believed I was not a bad person. Yes, I made mistakes, but I did not consciously "sin." I began to see that *every* thought, word, or deed in my life that was not in alignment with his Word was sin, regardless of whether intended or unintended. Being "sorry" with an infinite number of apologies did not equal repentance.

This was a revelation, not a condemnation. It did not matter whether I "meant" it or whether I "chose" it, or whether I was just plain "ignorant." The issue was whether I was in alignment with God. By acknowledging I was not in sync with the Word, I could get back into alignment with Him by repenting. No whining, no sweat of the brow, or prolonged punishment needed. Just the supernatural cross of Jesus Christ.

I began to see that when the actions and words of others, intentionally or unintentionally pushed me off course with God, it was my choice to forgive them, notwithstanding. If I were still holding on to any part of that offense, I had not fully forgiven. I grasped a new model for total forgiveness. Just saying, "I forgive them" or trying to "shake it off" or even speaking blessings did not work to set me free from offense. Phrases like "No big deal," "Don't worry about it," or "No problem" are excuses, not forgiveness. I had to accept "they owed me nothing—no restitution, no apology, no reasons, no explanations, and no excuses." I had to give up my right to any measure of restitution. That too is supernatural.

As I applied what I was learning, I slowly rose out of depression. I say, "sloooowly" as it took about two years for me to be stable and productive again. I had prided myself as a multi- tasker juggling many things at once. When depression set in, I could not function—practically, emotionally, or intellectually. I couldn't cook, pay bills, or do laundry. I couldn't hug my children or say to them "I love you." I couldn't think straight or remember what day it was. As I practiced repentance and forgiveness, the light of Christ slowly overcame the darkness in my soul. I discovered that the way of peace is through repentance and forgiveness as I am reconciled to God. He restored me to greater functionality and capability in life.

Prologue

In Luke 10:38-42, Martha invited Jesus for the first time to the home she shared with her sister Mary. Martha continued with "business as usual" making preparations for an honored guest resuming the tasks she probably always did. Because Mary was not helping, she complained to Jesus, "Lord, don't you care that my sister has left me to do the work by myself? Tell her to help me!" Jesus answered, "Martha, Martha, you are worried and upset about many things, but few things are needed—or indeed only one. Mary has chosen what is better, and it will not be taken away from her." (NIV) Mary's choice of sitting at his feet was a statement of priorities.

When you invite Jesus into your life (home), you cannot return to "business as usual." Your focus must shift from your daily busyness to His presence. "Sitting at his feet" is a form of acknowledging His presence. Spending time to listen and worship must become the new norm. Surely you are to continue in your daily duties like paying bills, house cleaning, and cooking meals but Jesus now becomes a priority. The balance of life shifts when Jesus joins the equation.

How To Use This Book

The basic format here involves interaction between a counselor and a client. The exercises can be repeated and the roles exchanged. The same format can also be used in a group setting with a leader or facilitator taking the role of a counselor. In a group setting, participants should write their answers instead of giving verbal responses. The group can benefit from the experiences if participants share at the end of the exercise.

> "For where two or three gather in my name, there am I with them." (Matthew 18:20)

> And the prayer offered in faith will make the sick person well; the Lord will raise them. If they have sinned, they will be forgiven. 16 Therefore confess your sins to each other and pray for each other so that you may be healed. The prayer of a righteous person is powerful and effective. (James 5:15-16)

Junkyard Treasure

The Man was walking through the junkyard looking for something he treasured. There it was! His first car his Dad gave to him. He was so excited to see it.

He ran to the junkyard owner and asked, "Is that car for sale?"

The owner questioned him, "Why do you want *that* thing? It's a mess—rusty, falling apart, not able to do what it was made for. It was in a few crashes. Not worth fixing."

"I don't care. How much?"

The owner rubbed his chin and with an evil eye quoted an outrageous price.

The Man said, "I'll take it" and paid the price.

The Man took the car home and made a plan to restore it to its original glory. He put it up on cinder blocks. The engine started with much grinding and sputtering. The Man painstakingly cleaned and restored the most vital sections of the engine. He put new tires on it and proudly took it for a spin around the neighborhood. The neighbors only saw a dilapidated car with dents, rust, broken glass, and a trashed interior. But, The Man knew that someday it would be the boast of the town.

The Man's mechanic friends joined Him working on his new project. Then more friends came to restore the interior with new seats, upholstery, and mats. They put in new windows and a new steering wheel. Finally, the last group of friends came to do bodywork. They scraped, sanded, and pounded out dents. They refitted parts, painted, and polished until it was a work of art. At every stage, The Man would drive his car around the neighborhood to show it off. Eventually, the neighbors looked forward to the drive around the block. They all cheered when He took it out on the first road trip.

Are you in a junkyard, battered and in disrepair? Jesus is The Man. He is looking for you because his Father gave you to Him. When he takes you into his garage, you will be on cinder blocks for a period. His friends will come to "work on you". Mechanics will work on how you think and behave. Interior restorers will work on your emotions, choices, and relationships. Bodyworkers will address your health and appearance.

The Lord will not leave you in a junkyard when you call out to him. He is waiting for your call. His "friends" are teachers, pastors, and doctors ready to work on you to restore you. Will you let them? They are under his watchful eye and direction.

Psalm 102:17 He will respond to the prayer of the destitute; he will not despise their plea.

The Great Exchange, The Story of Salvation

God grieved because mankind was lost to Satan through the disobedience of Adam and Eve.

Satan to God: "Ha! I got the humans you created and you thought they were so good!"

God to Satan: "Those are MY children. I want them back. I will give you gold and silver for each one you took."

"I know you own all the gold and silver in the earth, or least you *did*. You gave it all to mankind and now I can get all I want because they will give it to me." Satan replied sarcastically.

God declared, "They are more precious than all the gold or silver on earth."

"You know the rules! Restitution for sin has to be like for like. Adam & Eve were pure and holy. You can only get them back with another human pure and holy and there isn't anyone now or ever who will be from this stock. They are forever contaminated! There is no forgiveness without the shedding of blood!" Satan answered, in a voice of superiority.

God said with determination, "I'm going to buy them back with the flesh of mankind that is pure, without any trace of disobedience just like Adam had before he disobeyed. I will do whatever it takes."

"Good luck!" Satan retorted.

God, Jesus, and the Holy Spirit huddle in a conference.

Father God, "I am so grieved that my human children are lost."

Holy Spirit, "Should we destroy mankind and start all over again?"

Father said with resolve, "I can't. I won't! I love them too much. Besides, if I destroy them, I destroy myself and you, Holy Spirit, because I breathed my breath into them. I will not destroy mankind. I will redeem them.

First, I will find a man I can use to create a new nation. In faith, he will obey me to leave his homeland and family. It will take generations to bring redemption to the human race. To redeem mankind there must be a human born of flesh and blood who will obey me totally from birth to death."

Jesus, in excited anticipation, "Dad, you can do anything. Make me into a human and I will go."

Father protesting his son's offer, "You are my precious Son! I can't let you do this. You will have to leave the courts of heaven and live as a man on earth. Then you will have to die!"

Jesus, "Dad, you love them as much as you love me. Let me do it."

"Are you sure son? It's not going to be pretty as Satan is pretty gruesome," the Father said with hesitation.

"I'll do it, Dad, if you promise never to leave me or forsake me."

"I will never leave you or forsake you." Here's the plan. This will take some time but we have eternity."

"Let's keep it a secret so Satan won't discover our plan," whispered the Holy Spirit.

"No matter what happens, My people must know that I am working on their behalf so I will tell my prophets to prepare the people for a Savior. The plan will be veiled not secret. Men must know I love them. When the time is right, we will sneak Jesus into the earth through a human vessel," Father said in determination.

Father turning to the Holy Spirit, "Holy Spirit, your job is to sneak Jesus onto earth through a human vessel I have prepared. Her name is Mary."

Then turning to the Son, "You must be obedient to her and me no matter what happens to you. Your flesh must be kept pure, you must be consecrated, and your spirit must always be with me."

"Got it, Dad," Jesus said.

Meanwhile, Satan believed God would not be able to produce another Adam as he knows the flesh is weak and he can tempt weak flesh into anything either by guile or force.

Jesus came to earth through the womb of a woman as a human man to carry out his Father's commands impeccably. He demonstrated the character of God and did not let Satan waylay him either by temptation or force. He showed us what mankind was created to be. He only did what the Father did-healing, doing signs and wonders, preaching, performing miracles, and casting out demons, in addition to doing carpentry.

As Jews, Jesus and his apostles had been celebrating The

Passover all their lives. This was the third celebration with Jesus.

Jesus said, "I am eager to eat this Passover with you."

Jesus called them all together at the Passover table, "Ok guys, this is it. All the former Passover feasts were memorials of Moses in Egypt and rehearsals for remembering the deliverance of our people. Kill the lamb. Put the blood on the doorposts. Roast it entrails and all. Eat the flesh. Stay inside undercover. Death will pass over you. That was the old covenant.

"This is the New Covenant. This one is *not* a rehearsal. This is the first and last event of this kind. I am the Passover Lamb of God. When you eat this bread, it is the flesh of The Passover Lamb. My Flesh. See this wine? The juice from the grapes was squeezed out of the grape. This wine is My Blood that will be squeezed out of me. Drink this cup so we can be one.

"I want you to eat this bread and drink this cup to recall the power of Me in your lives and what I am about to do for you. We will be in communion. You and I will be one. I am going to take the hit/punishment of sin. You won't have to hide in shame anymore. When I rise, you will rise with me and together we will be victorious over death. Death will be under our feet."

At his last Passover Supper, Jesus says of the bread "this is my body" which is just like yours except it is uncontaminated by sin. Take it and eat it for the impact of what I am about to do for you. This wine is my blood which is uncontaminated by sin. When you drink it, you will be a child of my Father God, just like I am. I am his blood child. You will have all the inherited attributes of character, power, and authority released in you just as he has given me. When I return to the Father, do this to remember Me and what I am doing for you."

In the Garden of Gethsemane, Jesus said to the Father, "What did we say in the huddle? Let's go over this again. Isn't there some other way? What's Plan B? This looks ugly. But, if that's what we decided, that's what we will do. You said you will never leave me or forsake me."

The crucifixion of Jesus was so horrible that even **He** thought his Father had forsaken Him. He experienced the full impact of Satan's cruelty to mankind. He was condemned to death by the religious leaders for being the God who He was, and was traded by the world for the criminal he was not.

Satan did not believe God could provide pure, sinless flesh to exchange. He tortured Jesus to prove perfect obedience was impossible. Satan was wrong. God bought back all his children for all eternity with the flesh and blood of Jesus. He paid the price.

The Great Exchange, The Story of Salvation

The Old Covenant protects you from death.

The New Covenant allows you to overcome death.

The only thing on this earth powerful enough to remove sin is the Blood of Jesus. This great exchange is what salvation is all about. Salvation starts as a single event of accepting Jesus as Savior, but it is a life-long process to make Him Lord.

Repentance and forgiveness appropriate the Blood of Jesus to break the chains of sin that keep you from moving toward God. God does not expect you to be sinless since that privilege was lost in the Garden of Eden. He does call you to be holy and blameless by using the Blood of Jesus. Any chain of sin can be removed when you repent and forgive at the cross of Jesus. To repent and to forgive are the two supernatural choices for a Christian.

Jesus loves you. I am not parroting a Sunday school song. He is someone who went through crucifixion for you, not because you're worthy, earned it, or wanted it, but because He loves you. He wasn't killed. He chose to *give* his life up so you could live free from bondage and the shame of sin. This is something difficult to grasp until you start submitting your life to having every link of sin removed.

Chapter 1
Rescued From Eden's Exile

Break the Ball-and-Chain Existence

Whenever Bob got together with his buddies, they would share travel stories. Bob would only talk about his wife's travels.

"My wife just got back from Ireland. She's in Hawaii now to see her family." Bob chimed in.

"You should have gone with her. Hawaii is beautiful," Joe added.

"Naw. I like it at home. It's more comfortable. Anyway, she has so many relatives, it's a zoo when they get together," Bob said with irritation in his voice.

Several years later, "I just got back from Hawaii visiting my in-laws. It was a blast! The food is so great!" Bob told his buddies.

"Hooray! What took you so long to change your mind?"

"The truth is, I finally kicked smoking. Before this, I could not go more than two hours without a cigarette, so, I knew flying five hours on a non-smoking flight would have killed me. Now I'm free from chain-smoking I can go anywhere. Haven't picked up a cig in five weeks. I tried to quit so many times but this time it worked. I don't even want one. My wife is really happy!"

Cigarettes, alcohol, and drugs are the most common addictions acknowledged. Money, sexual pleasure, social media, and competition are less talked about. Addictions are a lure to fill an inner emptiness or to soothe emotional pain. It may soothe the pain but causes you to fail your other responsibilities such as your family, friends, and finances. You may think you are in control, but when you try to take a different route, you are trapped.

Addictions are often the tell-tale sign of inner bondage. Fear, rejection, and trauma are common bondages that keep you in a stalemate. The inability to get ahead financially, to build close friendships, or to hold on to a job bring angst. Some people mourn being estranged from their children, while others could not maintain good health despite special diets and nutrition plans. They tried their best, but all their efforts were somehow thwarted to reach the promises of prosperity in body, mind, spirit, pocketbook, and relationships as promised in the Bible. (Deuteronomy 28:1-14) These promises have conditions of obedience to His commands and these conditions are impossible to fulfill independent of God.

Sin subtly sneaks into your life to block God's blessings. When you exercise your free will toward sin, either knowingly or unknowingly, the devil can take advantage of you. He prefers you to act out of blindness or ignorance. Gossip might seem like fun, making you feel important for a moment. But since gossip hurts others, you have done the devil's dirty work for him and your integrity is compromised. When you repent and forgive, you permit God to remove the presence of the sin in your life. Without the stain of sin, you can quit gossiping.

A Second Chance to Succeed

God wants you to stay on track with Him so you can prosper in the spiritual and natural realms. Sin will disconnect you from God. It will derail you like a train with one wheel off the track that eventually comes to a grinding halt at best, or, flip off the track in a heap of twisted wreckage. Sin desensitizes your brakes and derails you. The train without brakes inevitably ends in a major crash with casualties. Sin enters your life through the choices you make or refuse to make. Sin also enters your life through another person's bad choice. Regardless of the source, the results will be the same. Train wreck!

Unfortunately, many Christians are unaware of the devil's schemes that prey on ignorance, innocence, pride, and rebellion. The devil wants God's glory for himself. He does not want your money, stuff, or even your life per se. He wants power from your worship and obedience. He will do whatever it takes to give God a bad rap. He will make you sick, depressed, or downtrodden so you pull away from God. Alternatively, he may make you wealthy, famous, and glamourous if that's what it takes to turn you away from God. The devil has no ethics, and he doesn't play fair. He will use anyone and anything to deter you from walking with God. He will even work through generations and those closest to you. But God has a destiny and purpose for you which He planned since the world began. When you fulfill that purpose, His plan for the earth can be accomplished. Not all God's purposes bring *you* glory, but His purposes always bring *Him* glory.

Obedience to God is of utmost importance even if His purposes are hidden from you. You may be a teacher for special needs kids or a teacher for today's geniuses. God puts a passion for them in your heart and also the skill in your hands to bring them through.

The Panama Canal

For years, many dreamed of a canal over the Isthmus of Panama to shorten the trade route from the Atlantic to the Pacific. Encouraged by the success of the Suez Canal in Egypt, a French endeavor began in 1881. Unfortunately, they were unprepared for the challenge of a dense jungle filled with snakes, insects, and mosquitoes. Workers were expected to live off the land. Rainy season mudslides were catastrophic. Thousands of workers died of yellow fever. Pans of water were set under the bedposts of infirmary cots to keep the "yellow fever carrying ants" away from patients. Yellow fever was being transmitted by mosquitoes, and those pans of water were the perfect breeding ground. The canal project was abandoned in 1889 after thousands of deaths and cost overruns.

Fifteen years later, in 1904, President Theodore Roosevelt saw the canal as a strategic necessity for the United States. He negotiated a deal for a US-controlled Panama Canal Zone. Realizing this project would take many years to complete, the U.S. Army Corps of Engineers built an infrastructure of housing, schools, hospitals, stores, and churches for workers on the canal project. Meanwhile, Dr. Walter Reed discovered the spread of yellow fever could be abated if the life cycle of the mosquito was interrupted. Swamps were drained, windows were screened, marshes oiled, and insecticides were sprayed. With the infrastructure in place and yellow fever abated, the Panama Canal project began again and this time met with success.

Your first attempt at living a fulfilling, God-ordained life on your own is fraught with flimsy infrastructure, traumas, and spiritual fever. Sin carries a death sentence regardless of whether the sin was committed by you or committed against you. Sin will cause you to abandon the project, take another path, or maybe even find life hopeless. It is through Jesus that the life cycle of sin is interrupted.

Take Action

Because you now have a Savior on your side to break the bondage of sin supernaturally, you need to know how to take action. Becoming a Christian is not just a "feel good" experience. It is not a club to join because your friends are Christians. You are not a Christian because you go to church. You become a Christian when you commit to living with Christ in your life.

Just as you learn how to use the apps on your phone you must learn to use the "Jesus app." The "Jesus app" includes repenting of your sins, forgiving others for sins against you, living by the Word of God, and building a relationship with Him.

One summer day, I was at the local street fair watching a demonstration of a super-absorbent cleaning cloth.

"Step right up folks. Take a look at what this miracle cleaning cloth can do," he said as he wrung it dry over a bucket. Then he poured a liter bottle of soda on the table-top. "Ever spill a drink on your coffee table and can't get it all up quickly with a towel? Watch this! Just put the cloth over the spill and in an instant, it will be completely absorbed. Best yet, when you clean windows, no water-marks! You will always have clean windows! I guarantee you will never have dirty windows again"

I bought the miracle cloth and put it in my cleaning equipment closet where it stayed for months. I continued to have dirty windows because I never used it. Could I say he gave an empty promise?

If you do not consistently practice repentance and forgiveness to remove sin from your life, you will continue to live in the consequences of sin and bondage of the devil. When you turn from the things of the world that marred you, the Lord does not discard you. He reshapes you into another vessel for His purpose. (Jeremiah 18:1-4) Just as the clay pot became marred as the potter was shaping it, the Lord will not discard you but will reshape you into another vessel.

Jesus told Nicodemus that there is a second chance at life through a rebirth of the spirit through faith in the Son of Man (Jesus) and the Holy Spirit. (John 3:5-13) You are empowered through the baptism of the Holy Spirit to use all the spiritual gifts that are given you to be successful. (1Corinthians 12:7-11). Righteousness, peace, and joy are marks of a Holy Spirit-filled life. (Romans 14:17)

The Great Escape

Unconfessed sin is anything you knowingly refuse to acknowledge as being out of alignment with God. Like the law of gravity, the law of sin and death is always in operation. If you are out of alignment with God, you are at risk of the consequences.

"Please forgive me," is *not* repentance. Asking the victim of your rock-throwing to forgive you is asking *him* to do something. Repentance concerns what *you* are to do. Your *decision* not to throw rocks again is the first step. Repentance happens when you change your behavior. Admit your wrongdoing and quit throwing rocks. The rocks can be literal rocks or rocks in the form of sarcastic remarks, judgments, or gossip. Saying "I'm sorry" is an emotional expression, not a life choice. Expressing sorrow with continued rock-throwing is not repentance. Repentance does not depend on whether your victim forgives you, it depends on *you*.

Another level of repentance includes bringing sin into the light, no longer letting shame or denial reign. For someone who is a victim of abuse, kidnapping, or rape, repenting means to *admit* such a thing happened and choose to allow Jesus to cleanse it from shame. Sinful reactions of resentment, hate, or bitterness that dwell in the heart can never be removed except through repentance. The victim mindset will say "It's not my fault," but the repentant mindset will say "I don't want to carry this throughout my life. I'm going to lay it down." Such a prayer would be like this.

"Lord I admit I have been a victim of (kidnapping). I now expose it to your cross to be set free from the sin of another against me. I also repent of any anger, resentment, self-condemnation, or shame that I have been holding in my heart from this event. I choose to forgive."

This kind of repenting does not change history but it does change the victim's relationship with the event. The pain and shame will be removed and the sin cycle is broken supernaturally.

There are three components to repentance: *Hands, Head, and Heart*. The *hands* are what you do. You could be destroying a poster, not showing up for a date, or robbing a bank. If you perceive someone is going to hurt you, your *head* plans a response. Finally, your *heart* stores resentment, judgment, and bitterness.

In the rock-throwing example, your hands threw the rocks, your head believed someone was going to hurt you, your heart harbored fear, anger, and even revenge. If your hands stop, but your head and heart are still festering, two-thirds of the sin continues. The chances are good that your hands will erupt again. But, if you repent of throwing rocks (hand) at your neighbor's house, and repent for stockpiling rocks to throw (head planning), and repent of holding a grudge (heart), y*ou* will be set free.

The depth of the repentance determines the depth of forgiveness. Here is an example of deeper repentance.

- I repent of being angry with my neighbor. (generic)
- I repent of yelling at my neighbor when he harassed my dog. (specific)
- I repent of holding in my heart resentment, hurt, bitterness, anger, and unforgiveness toward my neighbor because he harassed my dog and shouted obscenities at me. (clear and specific)

Your mind is so quick, that a thought can be repeated and embellished hundreds of times within a few seconds. When you are verbally clear and specific, you reduce the chance of nursing the details to keep it alive. When you can be specific on the point of anger, you have a greater chance of disengaging the anger. You can tear up the invisible scorecard.

Avoid the Traps

Falling into sin can happen so quickly that you don't know it just went through three stages—temptation, entertainment, and commitment.

1. *Temptation* is the thought, the emotional hit, and the unexpected jolt of an event that cracks open the door for a reaction. It is like being tripped. Something you fear, someone you don't like, or something you are trying to avoid sneaks up on you. You are tempted to take action either against them or yourself. Don't be caught off guard to the devil's schemes. In the Garden of Gethsemane Peter jumped to cut off the ear of the high priest's servant. (Matthew 26:51) Jesus told his disciples to pray and not fall into temptation.
2. Entertainment is thinking about, planning, and rehearsing an anticipated scenario. You plan your reaction. "The next time Bob touches the gate, I'm going to say: *%@ ." Usually your plan is a hurtful one. Constantly complaining or murmuring ends up in gossip, put-downs, and overall negativity. Entertaining sin can happen over five seconds or five years.
3. *Commitment* happens when you carry out the plan of sin you have entertained.

Your mind and emotions move so quickly that all three stages can happen in a split second. When you know your temptations or trigger points, you can disconnect before stepping into sin. If you don't know what your triggers are, ask trusted friends and the Holy Spirit to reveal them to you. Repent and forgive yourself for not being vigilant. Forgive those people the devil has used to entrap you.

The Great Release

When hurt and pain strike deep within your soul, unforgiveness festers there. You may believe you have forgiven, but all you did was discount the offense, while the hurt keeps you in chains. The chains of unforgiveness rob you of peace, and of the ability to build something new.

According to the Law of Restitution (Exodus 22), each offense deserves some kind of restitution for a debt to be satisfied. It is a "paid in full" receipt. As long as you are dealing with things that can be replaced, restitution and reparation are possible. However, if you suffer the loss of an arm, a job, or a loved one, restitution from the offender is impossible. Because the law of restitution cannot always be met, you try to rely on lesser versions of restitution, which may be apologies, reasons, explanations, or excuses.

An **apology** is a verbal admission of wrong-doing by the offender and a statement that he has remorse for causing hurt. Apologies do not restore. When the hurt is so damaging, an apology is not enough to satisfy. When pain persists, you may grapple with "you're not sorry enough" or the offending party will be forever apologizing never coming to peace. Sometimes an apology will not be forthcoming because the offender cannot or does not know there was an offense.

Reasons "why" is the next level your heart searches. Did you throw rocks at me because you hated me or because you didn't see me? Neither reason "why" would change the fact that I was hurt when the rock that you threw hit my eye. A reason does not restore my sight.

Explanations give information. You could talk about the trajectory of the rock, the force with which you threw it, and where I was standing before the rock hit my eye. None of that information restores my eye.

The **excuse** or blame-shifting to an outside cause is the final and weakest grasp for restitution. "I threw rocks because I didn't pass the exam" is blame-shifting. When you are desperate for something to grasp, you may make up excuses for others, such as "His father is an alcoholic," "She's having a bad day," and "She must have had an argument with her husband."

Use this formula: RAREX to be assured of total forgiveness. When you *choose* to give up your right to restitution you are set free to let God restore you.

For example: "I forgive Joni for throwing rocks at me and hurting my eye. She owes me nothing, no \ **restitution**—she does not have to make it up to me. She owes me no **apology**, no **reasons**, no **explanations**, and no **excuses**. I release her 100%."

By praying forgiveness this way, you quit holding on to any thread of unforgiveness on that issue. If each facet of forgiveness is released, all ties of the sin with the offender are then removed.

This is not always easy to do, especially when emotions are raw and the stakes are high. This is done by *choice* knowing that there will be freedom from constant pain. I would caution you not to rely totally on your emotions as you may never feel like forgiving and thus lose out on the precious peace that you will receive by forgiving.

As long as the offender is expected to provide restitution in any measure, unforgiveness will linger. When you let go 100% of your right to receive restitution, Jesus can step in to be your restitution, for He can restore to you what you lost and much more. He can restore your dignity, your prosperity, and even your sight. Remember, only the supernatural Blood of Jesus through repentance & forgiveness removes sin.

He Owes Me!

Chandler just bought for his son, Curtis, an ice-cream cone from the sweet shop at the amusement park. As they were leaving the store, a teenager rushed past them knocking the Curtis' ice-cream to the ground leaving him with only the cone in hand. He cried. Chandler yelled at the teen who, by then, disappeared with his friends. He probably didn't know what happened or didn't care.

"That careless kid must replace Curtis' ice-cream!

"Sir, I'll be happy to give Curtis another one. No charge," offered the clerk.

"I want that kid to get back here. Hey kid!! No, we won't take the free ice-cream."

At the ruckus, the manager came out. "What's happening? Can I help you, sir."

"That #$% kid knocked over my son's ice-cream and just ran off. He ought to get back here and pay for a replacement."

"I'm sorry that happened, sir. Sometimes those things

happen when there are so many people. Let me get your son a double scoop cone for the trouble."

"We don't want a double scoop ice-cream. We just need that kid to come back and pay for another one. That @#$ kid! Why don't they watch where they are going!" Meanwhile, passers-by look over at the scene.

Finally, Mr. Gibbins, the shop owner came out. "Sir, Sir, I am so sorry that happened. Let me give you and your son each a three-scoop Sunday with any toppings you'd like."

"Oh, you people are impossible! Come on Curtis, let's go. They don't want to go find the kid. We'll find him." He stomped away with his crying son.

This story, though exaggerated, illustrates how you can miss the goodness of God when you refuse to forgive insisting on restitution from the offender. When you forgive, you allow God to bless you double and triple times through the hand of others.

Don't Forget them

The three persons you may fail to forgive are institutions, yourself, and God. You live by perception more than by facts, and perceptions can steer you into choppy waters. **Institutions** are entities without a face or an accountable person you can identify who has sinned against you—the

Department of Motor Vehicles, an insurance company, or the hospital. Just because they are faceless, it does not mean you have not been hurt, so, it's important to forgive them too. Examples are: "I forgive the university for losing my grades." "I forgive the insurance company for dragging out my claim and requiring so much paperwork." Heart repentance is also required: "I repent of holding anger, resentment, and bitterness against the hospital pharmacy."

Forgiving the institution of the Church is critical to your relationship with God. If whoever is the face of the Church to you—a Pastor, an Elder, or fellow member—has offended you, forgive completely. If you are holding a grudge because the choirmaster did not assign you the solo, or the vestry did not approve your favorite project, forgive and repent of holding a grudge. If you have been abused by a church representative, still forgive. Although you are not required to submit to continued abuse, choose to repent and forgive then move out of harm's way. If you do not, you risk cutting off God and his blessings for you.

The second person to forgive is **you**. People say "I can never forgive myself" when they see themselves as having done something wrong. In utter frustration, a mom may say to her teenage son, "I don't want to deal with you again." The boy then runs away from home and sparks a massive manhunt. She will struggle to forgive herself for what she said to him, for being impatient, for not understanding him, etc. A parent who leaves children alone in the car while making a quick run into the store only to find harm came upon them, will self-condemn. You blame yourself for an accident when going hiking alone. All these situations are opportunities for constant self-condemnation in the heart. If you do not forgive yourself, you are in essence saying that you are greater than God. He promises to forgive all that we bring in repentance and forgiveness to the cross. Is your sin greater than God's ability to forgive? See yourself as the person who has offended you. Forgive yourself. Do it completely with RAREX.

The third person you fail to forgive is **God**. If you perceive that God has let you down by not coming through with what you wanted or when you wanted it, your heart will hold a grudge against Him. Holding unforgiveness toward God will cut you off from Him. You cannot fully receive from someone you are holding anger against. You will miss the fact that He still does all things for your benefit. You may believe you are waiting for God to answer your prayer while He is waiting for you to do your part to bring the answer. He cannot release wealth to you until you learn to steward your money and learn how to budget correctly on what you have so you can be trusted with more. He is waiting to heal your body as soon as you take steps to respect it and take care of it. He is still there being God, but a wall of unforgiveness stands between you and

Him. You are exalting yourself above him if you do not forgive him.

The Blessing comes

At 30 years old I was planning to become pregnant with our second child. My doctor discovered I had stage three cervical cancer. I believed God could have prevented cancer from attacking my body. I trusted him for good health, so I blamed Him for letting this happen. Activated hormones during pregnancy would accelerate the cancer spread. I would be able to bear a child but risked dying of cancer soon thereafter. I decided to have a hysterectomy and not take that risk. I was angry at God for taking my dream of bearing three children. I had to forgive God for allowing cancer to attack my body. God kept his promise to remove disease from my body through surgery and with no further treatment and no reoccurrence. Over the ensuing years, He brought two lovely children through adoption. My dream of having a family of three children was realized. It was not what I visualized but it was fulfilled none the less. God came through for me based on faith that He could do what He promised. (Psalm 113:9) "He settles the childless woman in her home as a happy mother of children."

Repentance and forgiveness are two sides of bondage-breaking currency. Either one alone is like a dollar bill printed only on one side. If you find yourself constantly forgiving and never being set free, do some repenting. Likewise, if you are always repenting and feeling like an underdog, begin forgiving. Both require a choice on your part. Where repentance is required, there always is forgiveness waiting to be addressed.

Chapter 2
Be Strong and Take Heart

Wait for the LORD; be strong and take heart and wait for the LORD. (Psalm 27:14)

No More Band-Aids

A simple definition of wholeness is, "nothing missing, nothing broken." A broken heart is real, not imaginary. Traumatic life events, negative beliefs, and crushed emotions will cripple you with a broken heart. Although your body can still function without certain organs, the vital organs must function to be alive. Jesus proclaimed Isaiah 61:1 as he began his ministry. "The Spirit of the Sovereign Lord is on me because the Lord has anointed me to proclaim good news to the poor. *He has sent me to bind up the brokenhearted*, to proclaim freedom for the captives and release from darkness for the prisoners." "He heals the wounds of every shattered heart." (Psalm 147:3)

Trauma is a sudden or unexpected event with overwhelming psychological, emotional, and sometimes physical impact. The event can throw you into confusion, emotionally paralyzing you. Some people lose their memory of the event and some are in constant fear of it. Multiple traumas cause multiple fractures in the heart. A trauma event can be as dramatic as being involved in

an auto accident, witnessing a murder, or being on a war battlefield. Yet a seemingly minor event such as attending the first day of kindergarten, or as a toddler getting lost in a grocery store, can be equally traumatic. Similar events later in life will have the same impact as did the original event. If the first day of school was traumatic, each first day of school thereafter may bring fear. In your adult life, the first day on a job could evoke the same kind of fear.

Any childhood experiences of physical abuse, serious illness, or emotionally overwhelming events such as the death of a parent, will fracture your soul. Brokenness makes you ineffective. In the effort to compensate, you

- devise defense mechanisms,
- build disconnecting behaviors,
- develop blind spots

- become easily distracted,
- have difficulty making decisions,
- have fearful thoughts based on "what ifs."

God does not want you crippled this way. Psalm 23 shows you wholeness. "The Lord is my shepherd, I shall not want. He makes me lie down in green pastures; he leads me beside still waters; he restores my soul. He leads me in right paths for his name's sake."

According to the psalm, God's plan for you is:

- green pastures, not sparse, dried up places to graze
- still waters, not a life turmoil and strife
- full ability to walk in righteous paths and godly living
- restoration from injury or brokenness.

God wants to restore you to wholeness so you can interact with Him. He created you, so He knows how to repair you. Jesus is beyond time as we know it. He is the same yesterday, today, and forever (Hebrews 13:8) therefore He can reach into your past, heal it, bring it into your present, and have it serve your future. He does not change your history but supernaturally changes your connection to it. When you are restored to wholeness you will become more aware of who God created you to be. You no longer will be disjointed, anxious or broken.

"The Lord is compassionate and gracious, slow to anger, abounding in love." (Ps 103:8) He wants to heal you, not exacerbate your traumas. Trauma causes cracks in you as in a fragile cracked vase. Just because the pieces did not break apart completely, does not mean there is no pain. This condition can be healed through prayer without you re-living the traumas.

If you are to ready to "let go" of old memories without reliving them, then healing can come. It is important that you feel comfortable and safe in the process. The role of a prayer counselor is to guide you through, without giving advice or judging. Counselors must keep confidentiality at all times. "Submit to one another out of reverence for Christ." (Ephesians 5:21) Since Jesus has been with you throughout your life, his presence is important. The Holy Spirit will be active to reveal what needs healing and order the details of your life. Jesus' first word of his ministry was "Repent" (Matthew 3:2, Mark 1:15) and the last word was "forgive." (Luke 23:34) Repentance is acknowledging things are not on track with God. Repentance is *not* fault finding or blaming. It acknowledges what "is." Likewise, forgiving means admitting you suffered hurt at the hand of another and got off track with God as a result. Forgiving is not saying that what happened was acceptable or good.

Be Strong and Take Heart

As a victim of betrayal or abuse, you choose to forgive because you do not want to live with a sin based connection. You can still pursue justice even if you give up restitution. No condemnation against you can exist when you are in Christ Jesus by repenting and forgiving. (Romans 8:2) Repentance and forgiveness are life choices.

To help you to start your healing process to wholeness, read the example of a prayer session with someone I'll call "Jane."

Counselor: Holy Spirit, we invite you to lead us in this prayer time.

Jane, are you comfortable and ready for an adventure? If you imagine pictures, hear sounds or words, or have any special emotions come up, tell me about them. You do not have to interpret it or understand them. Let's start. "Holy Spirit, please remind Jane of a time, at any age, when she was happy."

Jane: I am five years old.

Counselor: What are the surroundings?

Jane: I am skating in front of grandma's house.

Counselor: Do you feel safe?

Jane: Yes.

Counselor: Is Jesus there somewhere in the picture?

Jane: He's here.

Counselor: Where is He and what is He doing?

Jane: He's standing to the side, watching me skate.

Counselor: Can you go up to him and stand next to him?

Jane: Now we are sitting together on the bench looking at each other.

Counselor: Do you feel safe with Jesus?

Jane: Yes. Now I am sitting on his lap. I like him.

Counselor: I'm going to invite other younger Janes who would like to come to sit with Jesus. "I'm inviting any young Janes ages three and four who want to come to sit with Jesus."

Jane: There are two. (These are emotional fractures.)

Counselor: OK. Let them sit with you and Jesus.

"I'm inviting any Janes younger than three to come. (Pause) Lord, I am asking for angels to help those young ones too little to come on their own. (Pause) Lord, please let angels escort those who are afraid."

Jane: There were four.

Counselor: "Now I am inviting any Janes between the age of 6 and 8 to come to this safe place with Jesus. "

Be Strong and Take Heart

Jane: Here come two.

Counselor: Let them sit on the bench with you and Jesus. "I am inviting and Janes between the ages of 9-12 years old."

Jane: One is running toward us.

Counselor: "I am inviting any Janes between ages 13 to 18. If there are any afraid, I'm saying to you this is a safe place. You can come without being afraid. No one is going to harm you."

Jane: Four are coming slowly

Counselor: Now I'm inviting Janes between the ages of 18 and 22.

Jane: There are two.

Counselor: Are there any between the ages of 22 and 30 who would like to join the group?

Jane: I see four.

Counselor: I'm inviting any between the ages of 30 and 40.

Jane: There is one.

Counselor: Are there any from age 40 to present?

Jane: None

Counselor: Is everybody there?

Jane: There's a whole group of us. The bench got bigger.

Counselor: "I am again inviting anyone who heard the invitations but did not come."

Jane: No new ones.

Counselor: Are you still five years old sitting on Jesus' lap with all the others around you?

Jane: Yes

Counselor: Repeat this prayer: "Lord I forgive all who have caused me to be broken. " (Jane repeats.) "I release them now. " (Jane repeats) "I repent of any sin of mine that brought brokenness into my life." (Jane repeats)

Counselor: "As you have repented and forgiven, the sins are now forgiven."

Counselor: Look to Jesus and say to him, "Jesus I want to be whole. Please put me back together again."

Jane: Jesus, I want to be whole. Please put me back together again.

Counselor: Just watch what happens. Tell me what you see.

Jane: All the people slowly melted inside of me. (Pause) Now I am the age I am now: 45.

Counselor: Where is Jesus?

Be Strong and Take Heart

Jane: He's standing next to me.

Counselor: Look at him and thank him.

Jane: Jesus, thank you for making me whole.

Here are some of the experiences described to me.

- Instantly everybody got sucked into me like a vacuum cleaner and now I am myself as now, feeling peace.
- One by one, the people are stepping inside of me.
- I don't know. I just feel different. Now I'm grown up. I am beautiful!

Process for Wholeness Prayer

The prayer process shown in the example above is effective in bringing wholeness to your fractured soul. A prayer partner can fill the Counselor role. If this format is unfamiliar to you and the Counselor, use the Counselor in the example above and put your name in place of "Jane." I recommend the Prayer Counselor keep notes of the answers. Allow at least an hour or more as this is not a "quickie" prayer.

If you want to use this format in a small group setting of 2-6, one person should fill the role of the Prayer Counselor. Be in a private place that is comfortable and well lighted. Remove all distractions of television, phones, or vocal background music. The Prayer Counselor is to remain quiet as Subjects write their answers. In this setting, the Subjects should write their answers to the questions to keep the process confidential. Subjects should follow the Counselor without the book.

Prayer Session

Counselor: "Do you feel safe and comfortable?" (*This is important to set the tone of the prayer session.*)

All: "Holy Spirit we invite you to lead the way and give revelation during this time of prayer."

Counselor: "Holy Spirit let (Name / each person) see themselves at any age when she/they were happy.

Subject: (*Say or write the age and describe the scene.*) *Counselor*: Lord, we invite you to be in this scene. *Subject*: Give or write a description.

> *If the Subject does not feel safe or is distracted, do not continue. Invite the presence of the Lord. If there still is fear or uneasiness, stop. It could mean this is not the time nor the place nor the right combination of people for this prayer. Choose another time that is free of distractions and time constraints. If Subject(s) are settled and comfortable, continue.*

Be Strong and Take Heart

Counselor: "I invite young (__name__) between the age of (__the vision and younger__) to come to join (__name__) and Jesus."

Subject:Tell or Write the number of persons arriving. Wait until all persons of that age arrive. Describe if there is something unusual.

Counselor: I now invite younger ones to come to this safe place where Jesus is. Lord send angels to bring any that are too young to come on their own.

1. *Keep inviting younger ones until the time of birth.*
2. *Start inviting ones from the age of the memory going upward in increments of 2-3 years until adulthood about age 20.*
3. *Invite persons in increments of 5 years until they are their current age. Take each step slowly. Keep the subject engaged by asking for responses of each age. There may be some tears. If there is too much anxiety or fear, stop. Thank the Lord for His presence and speak peace to the Subject. End the session gently.*
4. *If you proceed to the current adult age, when all persons are there, extend another general invitation to be sure everybody who wants to come is there.*

Counselor: I'm now inviting anyone who wants to come to join the group who hasn't come yet.

Instruct Subject: (repeat)I forgive all those who caused me to fracture and I repent of any sin of mine that brought fracture to my soul.

Counselor: As you have repented and forgiven, the sins are forgiven.

Subject: Jesus I want you to make me whole.

Counselor: (Pause) What is happening?

Subject: Describe or, if in a group, write. Each experience is different. If working with a group, have each write what was happening to them.

Subject: Thank you Lord for making me whole. I want to keep walking in wholeness.

Counselor: "Lord I pray for (name/ these here) that she/they may continue to walk in your presence in the days ahead. Amen."

Things to remember in prayer for supernatural wholeness.

1. Always and only proceed when in a safe and comfortable environment.
2. Invite Jesus to be present and so no fear can hamper the process.

Be Strong and Take Heart

3. Let the Holy Spirit lead.
4. After all persons are present, repent/admit the hurt. Forgive all.
5. Ask to be made whole.
6. Commit to walking in wholeness.
7. Close with thanksgiving and blessing.

It's An Inside Job

(Psalm 30:11) You turned my wailing into dancing; you removed my sackcloth and clothed me with **joy**.

There are 187 references to joy in the Bible. The people shout with joy, dance for joy, rejoice, and clap with joy. Everyone has been created with the capacity for joy. This includes you and all the grumpy people around you.

Joy is not to be confused with happiness. Happiness is based on circumstances. You are happy because I came to your birthday party. You are happy because you won first place for the best travel photo. When the circumstances change, you may no longer be happy. Joy, however, comes from inside your spirit. Even if I didn't come to your birthday party, you may still be joyful. You didn't win the prize, but you can still be joyful. You can be joyful while going through hardships. You have an abundant capacity for joy inside of you. "The joy of the Lord is your strength." (Nehemiah 8:10)

As a fruit of the spirit, joy is based on your relationship with God, rather than your circumstances. You can choose to activate joy at any time in your life. You have a "joy box" inside of you. God created your joy box to give you strength. The health of your "joy box" will determine your ability to access joy. A damaged joy box keeps God outside of your life if you cannot believe God cares for you, loves you, and sets boundaries for your future.

When your joy box is shut down, life is dreary and wearisome. If relatives, school mates, or neighbors put you down when you were joyous about something, you shut down to avoid being hurt. It might have been small or silly, but because it was important to *you*, you chose to hide your joy. Skipping school, rebelling against your parents, and carrying a cocky attitude lead to poor life choices that contaminate the joy box. Self-accusing thoughts that you are ugly, stupid, or clumsy could crowd out your joy. Life choices that brought dire consequences such as revenge, murder, or suicide will destroy your joy box. A dysfunctional joy box was either shut down, contaminated, or crowded out.

Renew and activate your "Joy Box, " a visual exercise

The following exercise is designed to walk you through the steps of restoring your joy box. Restoration is bringing it to the way it is should be now, not what it used to be. You can use the exercise to update your joy box at different stages in your life. Be prepared to write what you see, hear, and feel. Pause between questions giving time to carefully consider the answers.

First assess the condition of your joy box. How badly damaged is it? Second, take inventory of what's in it. Sin will contaminate it. When you take responsibility for damaging and contaminating the joy box, you can repent. Forgiveness is required to release others who caused damage or contamination.

Joy Box Prayer Ministry

Counselor: "Ask God to show you what *your* joy box is like."

1. What does it look like? (color, décor, shape, size)
2. Can you open it? Does it have a lock?
3. Is it broken? How?
4. What's inside? Good things or junk?
5. What does the inside look like?
6. Bring it to God for restoration.

Prayer over any or all listed below. "I repent for:

- shutting down my joy box to avoid hurt.
- collecting junk of rebellion, disrespect, and cockiness in my joy box.
- putting self-condemning attitudes and hopelessness into my joy box.

- smashing my joy box with murderous and suicidal thoughts, and self-criticism
- keeping God out of my joy box by refusing to acknowledge Him."

"I forgive those who came against my joy box. Especially those who:

- Shut down my joy box with criticism and judgment.
- Put junk in my joy box by encouraging rebellion, disrespect, and bad judgment.
- Filled my joy box with condemnation and hopelessness.
- Smashed my joy box with murderous words and cursing.
- Lured me away from God.

"Lord, please restore and activate my joy box." Wait and watch what happens.

- "Lord, I ask you to repair my joy box."
- "Lord, I ask you to fill my joy box with your treasures."
- "Lord, I ask you to expand my joy box to fill my life."

- "Lord, I ask you to pour your strength and presence into my joy box."

Counselor: "Lord, you said that whenever we repent and forgive You forgive us and put the sin away. These have repented and forgiven so now we ask for restoration of the joy box. In Jesus name, I activate your joy box to function the way it was created to be. Amen."

Describe what happened after this prayer.

Joy Box stories that have been shared

Eve

I didn't see a box. I saw a porpoise flailing in the water trying to swim with only one flipper up. As we prayed through the

repentance and forgiveness, the porpoise started to become upright and by the end of the prayer, it was swimming freely. When the joy box was activated, it started to leap out of the water and spinning like they do in the ocean.

Be Strong and Take Heart

Christie

During the break, I kept trying to imagine what my joy box could look like (I like to read ahead). I imagined the box as purple and fun. When you asked God to show us our joy box, mine ended up being completely different than I had imagined. It was a large gold rectangle with some type of sequins all over it. The lid was open like a clamshell and there was a big gold bow on top. I could see myself looking over the side of the box and could see that it was empty inside. The interior sides about a quarter of the way down were of gold satin but then it turned black almost like an elevator shaft. The box was infinite. At this time you began saying that some people's boxes might be shattered or smashed. I remember thinking well mine appears to be perfect and not thinking it needed anything. God always surprises! Once God began to change the boxes and make them perfect, the dark interior walls began to be whitewashed by a possible angel. As the walls became white, liquid gold started to overflow from the top of the box and now it was fully open. When you mentioned strength coming back into the box I saw tons of little character- like bicep emoticons being dropped in. Once all the biceps stopped falling in, a humongous firework display came out of the box with the liquid gold still flowing out. It was amazing to witness and definite proof that God is extravagant.

Jeniffer

I saw a plain box made of wood. It was sealed up, with no cover, no lock, or opening of any kind. As we prayed through the exercise the box became more elaborate and decorated beautifully. I suddenly realized the box was me. I am a joy to the Lord.

Leave the Old, Welcome the New

Every spring, there are new leaves on the trees. The old leaves don't stay for the next year. Even evergreens shed leaves at some time. God is not static. He is always renewing things. "Behold I make all things new." (Revelation 21:5)

Choosing to leave the old and cleave to the new will bring you the freedom to make new choices without old hindrances. Choosing new things requires a measure of risk. Comfortable and familiar mindsets, habits, and convenience often get in the way. With your fractured soul restored and your joy box revived, you now have greater freedom to exercise your free will in leaving and cleaving. To leave is to "detach from," and to cleave is to "attach to." Making the choice to leave something old is as important as choosing to move into something new.

Have you ever tried sitting on a chair without getting up from the one you're already sitting on? How about going to another room without leaving the one you're in? It's impossible. Holding on to the past is like facing backward while trying to walk forward. Jesus said, "No one who puts a hand to the plow and looks back is fit for service in the kingdom of God." (Luke 9:62) In other words, "Don't walk forward while looking back." New Year's resolutions try to put new behaviors on top of old mindsets. "Leaving and cleaving" requires you to leave behind old conflicts, old behaviors, old thinking, and even old relationships to make changes successfully. If you enter into marriage without leaving the single life behind, a dedicated marriage cannot emerge. You leave situations not because they were bad, but because you want to make room for the new season.

Once you leave and cleave, you are free to choose either to step forward on a new path or return to the old one. It's your choice. To choose to follow the path God has for you is the one that will bring you to your destiny and greatest joy. The prayers that accompany this section include repenting and forgiving of sin for any conflict that was not resolved in the past, known or unknown, done or left undone, intentionally or unintentionally. The following prayers will also include the choice to follow the ways of God through Jesus Christ. Jesus Christ is the one who restored wholeness to your soul and revived your "joy box." He is the one who knows how to lead the way to the new life.

This exercise requires physical movement. If you are doing self-directed prayer, set two chairs side by side about five feet apart, facing the same direction. One chair will represent the "old" and the other the "new." The examples and prayers are written out to facilitate a self-directed prayer time. Address each issue in the order given. Sit in the "old" chair, repent and forgive, to remove the conflict that was set in place because of any sin, whether you are aware of it or not—known and unknown. This sets you free to move on to the next phase of life. Move to the "new" chair and declare you are choosing to bring the new thing under the Lordship of Jesus Christ. Several issues will be addressed. Not all may pertain to you. It is best to address them in order as they are in the order of primary relationships. Read through all the issues for the examples that might stir some thoughts you had not considered. Pray through the ones that impact your life.

If this is a group exercise, a leader will direct the prayers and the movement from the "Old" chair to the "New" chair. Each person should have a seat in rows or a circle so that all can move simultaneously either to the right or left. If an issue does not pertain to you, just move with the others to keep the flow going. If the issue does not apply to anyone in the group, then the leader should move on to the next. At each pause, listen to the Holy Spirit to reveal anything that needs to come to the light.

1. Father and Mother

In early November, an agitated woman in her forties confided she dreaded going to her Mom and Dad's home for the Thanksgiving holiday.

"Oh, how I dread going there!" "Why do you go?"

"I have to. Everybody in the family will be there and expect me."

"How far is it?"

"It's a 3-hour drive of clenching my teeth and gripping the steering wheel. Every mile fills me with apprehension!"

"What are you thinking on this drive?"

"I hear old conversations that exhaust me. I like visiting with the aunts and cousins but when I get there, I can't wait to leave."

"Let's pray the leave and cleave prayer. Repeat after me."

Lord, I forgive my mother and father for their negative interactions with me and my husband and child. I forgive them for any sin against me at any time. I repent of holding anger, resentment, and judgment against them in any way. I now choose to leave my old relationship with mom and dad, and cleave to a new relationship with them."

In our prayer time, she repented of keeping all the old anger and hurts from childhood, teenage years, and adult years. She forgave them for their negative interaction with her husband and her child. She was ready to leave and cleave to Jesus as Lord.

The next month she reported to me that the Thanksgiving gathering was different. She went just as she had before but she was not in turmoil and not anxious to leave the moment she got there. In fact, to her surprise, she was among the last to leave. She enjoyed seeing everyone, including Mom and Dad. Mom and Dad did not change, but she had changed and her relationship with them was without strife.

PRAYER:

Sit in the "old" chair and say, "I repent of my sin against my father and mother. (Pause to state anything specific that comes to mind.) I forgive my father and mother for any sin against me. (Pause to speak out any specific thing that you remember.) They do not have to make it up to me —no restitution, no apology, no reasons, no explanations, no excuses. I release them 100%." (Pause) *Get up from the "old" chair and move to the "new" chair.*

Declare: "I choose to leave my old relationship with father and mother, and move to a new relationship with my father and mother under the Lordship of Jesus Christ."

2. **Ex-significant-other, ex-spouse, or the deceased spouse**

Do this exercise separately for *each* ex-significant-other, ex- spouse, or even a deceased spouse. If the past relationship was bad, you will want to do this. However, you *leave* old relationships, not because they were bad, but because you want to be free to *cleave* to a new one with a fresh start. It's time to leave the longing for "the one you wish you married," or even "the one you dated for 12 years." It's important to leave a deceased spouse so that you can have a fresh relationship with a new spouse or a prospective new spouse. Even a good former relationship can restrict freedom in a new relationship. This will free you from living in the past. Leaving a former relationship means it's time to move on. Make the same movement from the "old chair" to the "new chair."

PRAYER:

"I repent of any sin against (__name__). (Pause)

I forgive (__name__) for any sin against me. (Pause) He/she does not have to make it up to me—no restitution, no apology, no reasons, no explanations, no excuses. I release him/her 100%." (Pause)

Get up from the chair and move to the "new" chair.

Declare: "I choose to leave my old relationship with (_name_) and move to my new relationship with (_name_) with Jesus Christ as Lord."

3. **Current spouse or significant other**

Within my 46 years of marriage, I have gone through several seasons with my husband in which our relationship changed. The early years were focused on career building then child-rearing, followed by financial pressures to educate them. As empty-nesters, we had to find out who we were as adults with adult children, and as retirees, we needed to discover our new purpose as elders in the community. "Leaving and cleaving" is equally important when transitioning from season to season.

PRAYER:

(Make the same movements from chair to chair.)

"I repent of any sin against (_name_). (Pause)

I forgive (_name_) for any sin against me. (Pause)

He/she does not have to make it up to me—no restitution, no apology, no reasons, no explanations, no excuses. I release him/her 100%."

Get up from the chair and move to the "new" chair.

Declare: "I choose to leave my old relationship with and move to my new relationship with (_name_) with Jesus Christ as Lord.

4. **Children (name them)**

Rearing children can be daunting. For them to come into their destiny, you must let them go. Pray this for each child individually to establish a healthy relationship with each. Old hurts and grudges with formerly difficult teenagers will keep you from enjoying them as adults. Your relationship with each child will be better when you release them through repentance and forgiveness. If you have no children of your own but have close ties with one that you consider to be like a son or daughter, you can also pray this for your relationship with them.

PRAYER:

"I repent of any sin against (_name_). (Pause)

I forgive (_name_) or any sin against me. (Pause)

He/she does not have to make it up to me—no restitution, no apology, no reasons, no explanations, no excuses. I release him/her 100%."

Get up from the chair and move to the "new" chair.

Declare: "I choose to leave my old relationship with (__name__) and move to my new healthy relationship with (__name__) with Jesus Christ as Lord.

5. **Friends:**

Your circle of friends changes because of moving away, business obligations, or just seasons of life. Frequently, close high school friends grow apart as they pursue careers. Married friends grow apart from single ones because their lifestyles have changed. You have the chance to move on to the next phase of your life and be blessed by the new friends without condemning old friendships.

My husband and I enjoyed the company of friends with whom we traveled and shared theatre outings. As our children grew to the age of involvement in soccer games, dance lessons, and scouts, we were no longer available to enjoy Saturday matinees at the theater. We were in a new season of our lives so we had to part ways as theater companions.

PRAYER:

"I repent of any sin against (__name__). (Pause)

I forgive (__name__) for any sin against me. (Pause)

He/she does not have to make it up to me—no restitution, no apology, no reasons, no explanations, no excuses. I release them 100%."

Get up from the chair and move to the "new" chair.

Declare: "I choose to leave my old relationship with (__name__) and move to my new relationship with (__name__) with Jesus as my Lord and savior."

6. **Job, business partner, and workplace**

Do this exercise for each job, workplace, or business partner with whom you have affiliated. If you can name the people involved, do so. However, remember a school district or an insurance company is a faceless entity even if there is a representative. Treat this "company" as if it were a person. Have you hurt them by your talk of disdain or disrespect? Likewise, were you hurt by its policies, rules, and regulations. You will be released from being mentally or emotionally stuck in the old job regardless of whether it was good or bad

I was a music teacher for 14 years in a local school district. Although I decided to end my teaching career to care for my children, my heart kept longing for the teaching days. The difficult transition was just a burden on my happiness. I had to leave being a career teacher and cleave to being a career mom.

PRAYER:

"I repent of any sin against (_company_). (Pause)

I forgive (_company_) for any sin against me. (Pause)

It does not have to make it up to me—no restitution, no apology, no reasons, no explanations, no excuses. I release them 100%."

Get up from the "old" chair and move to the "new" chair.

Declare: "I choose to leave my old relationship with (_company_) and move to my new relationship with (_company_) with Jesus Christ as Lord.

7. **Former to current residence**

When we leave a house, neighborhood, or city, emotional attachments make embracing the new place difficult. We long for the old grocery store, our long time doctor, and maybe even the weather. This exercise will help you to leave behind longing for what was good as well as any bad memories of a former residence. If you have moved many times, do the exercise for each move until you are settled in your current place.

I grew up in Hawaii, and am familiar with everything about Hawaiian hospitality. I attended graduate school in Illinois, intending to return to Hawaii. My heart and mind always went to Hawaii. When I married, my husband and I decided to make our home in California. My attachment to Hawaii had to fade away. Although we visit Hawaii often, the "place where I belong" needed to change to California so I could move into my future. It was time to leave Hawaii and cleave to California.

PRAYER:

"I repent of any sin against (_city_). (Pause)

I forgive (_city_) for any sin against me. (Pause)

It does not have to make it up to me—no restitution, no apology, no reasons, no explanations, no excuses. I release them 100%." (Pause)

Get up from the chair and move to the "new" chair.

Declare: "I choose to leave my old relationship with (_city_) and move to my new relationship with (_city_) with Jesus Christ as Lord.

8. **Church/worship**

God positions us to where we can be blessed and we can bless others. If you have been in the same church for more than 10 years, it's time to renew your church community relationship to be sure Jesus is Lord and you are called to be there. Jesus has always been a proponent of moving with God. The Pharisees and elders got so upset with him because he was trying to lead them into a new relationship with God but they were stuck in their familiar ways. God is always on the move to take us deeper with Him. As you mature in your spiritual journey, you need to update your church community. This does not mean you should change churches. It means you need to renew your calling in the church. You might consider making a shift from teaching Sunday School to serving on the home visitation group, or the Outreach ministry. God does not want you to be stagnant, especially in His Church. Do this exercise on your place in your church community. Leave the old and cleave to the new in the Lord's house.

After 10 years in a church where our children were nurtured and we shared life with many families like ours, the Lord moved me to a spirit-filled church experience. I stayed in the same denomination but found a spirit-filled church where I could grow in my spiritual journey. To embark on this new adventure, I had to leave the familiar setting and enter the new one to become a part of it. Each time the Lord called me to another place, to grow in my spiritual adventure, I had to leave what became familiar to enter a new community.

PRAYER:

"I repent of my sin against (_church_). (Pause)

I repent of any resentment, anger, judgment, or unforgiveness I may be holding against the leadership or community of my church.

I forgive(_church_) for their sin against me. (Pause) They do not have to make it up to me—no restitution, no apology, no reasons, no explanations, no excuses. I release them 100%." (Pause)

Get up from the chair and move to the "new" chair.

Declare: "I choose to leave my old relationship with (_church_) and move to a new relationship with (_church_) with Jesus as my Lord and savior.

9. **Finances**

Leave behind any financial mismanagement which hindered your prosperity.

For 12 years I worked in the mortgage department of a large bank. Loan applications were rejected because the credit report showed a lack of financial integrity even though the earnings were sufficient. Applicants failed to repay their student loans, their utility bills, and credit card bills on time. Are your funds being eaten up by late fees, bank penalties, or high-interest rates which all could have been avoided had you been more vigilant in handling your money? Do you have an emergency fund? Can you discern your wants from your needs? As in the parable of the talents (Matthew 25:14-30), those who know how to make prospering decisions will be rewarded.

PRAYER:

"I repent of my sin in finances. I repent of (_list them: not paying bills on time, spending more than I have, misusing credit cards, not repaying loans, and any other financial irresponsibility on my part_). (Pause)

I forgive myself for failing financial integrity. I forgive anyone who has caused me financial hardship. (Pause)

They do not have to make it up to me—no restitution, no apology, no reasons, no explanations, no excuses. I release them 100%." (Pause)

Get up from the chair and move to the "new" chair.

Declare: "I choose to leave my old way of handling finances and move to new ways with integrity with Jesus Christ as Lord.

10. **Health**

It is general knowledge that smoking, recreational drugs, and alcohol drinking are bad for your health. Problems of obesity, heart disease, and lung disease all connect to unhealthy lifestyles. Exercising, proper sleep, and diet are important for your body. Your body is meant to be the expression of God therefore leave your old unprofitable health habits, and cleave to new healthy ways of living.

I was a strong, active woman at age 65, or so I thought. I was able to do the chores around the house, take care of grandchildren, and still travel. However, I was gaining weight, and my energy level was dropping. I attributed it all to "getting old." One day it became very clear to me that *real* exercise was important if I wanted to continue an active life. I first joined the local gym and reached a certain level of self-directed fitness. At age 68, I was getting weaker, not stronger. My son introduced me to Crossfit. I could not run 100 meters without gasping for breath; I could not lift more than 10 pounds without straining; nor could I do sit-ups. I repented of my old ways of thinking about fitness and pushed on with Crossfit. I am more fit now than I was 20 years ago. I can carry my suitcase and run through an airport! I plan to be strong for another 25 years.

PRAYER:

"I repent of my sin against my health by (overworking, not resting, bad diet, lack of exercise, not following doctor's advice, etc. (Pauses)

I forgive myself for my sin against my body. (Pause)

I do not have to make it up to me—no restitution, no apology, no reasons, no explanations, no excuses. I release them 100%." (Pause)

Get up from the chair and move to the "new" chair.

Declare: "I choose to leave old health habits and exercise a new healthy lifestyle with Jesus Christ as Lord.

This "leave and cleave" prayer can be modified to address any situation you want to change. Continue to use the chairs as a visual act and apply the prayers to the following subjects.

Leave murmuring and complaining, cleave to thanksgiving. "I repent of murmuring and complaining.

I now choose to leave murmuring and complaining and cleave to thanksgiving with Jesus Christ as Lord."

Leave the judging and criticizing others, cleave to forgiveness. "I repent of judging and criticizing others with my opinion.

I choose to cleave to forgiveness with Jesus Christ as Lord."

Leave making excuses, blaming others, and professing self-justification. Cleave to repentance.

"I repent of making excuses, blaming others, and justifying myself.

I choose to cleave to responsibility for my actions with Jesus Christ as Lord."

Make these declarations.

I choose to walk supernaturally in freedom.

Jesus Christ has set me free, I am free indeed.
(John 8:36)

Where the spirit of the Lord is, there is freedom.
(2 Corinthians 2:17)

Chapter 3
Blessings For a Thousand Generations

Both medical and psychological sciences agree that generational influences through DNA impact your life. Twins or siblings who have been separated at birth have a strong affinity to one another regardless of separate life experiences. A combination of family talents plus a nurturing environment may be passed on through generations as evidenced in the Mozart familywithLeopold,andhischildrenMariaAnna and Wolfgang. Generations of pastors have filled pulpits, and artists such as the Wyeth family have graced homes and museums with their work.

God is a God of generations. Throughout the Bible, God refers to Himself as the God of Abraham, Isaac, and Jacob. (Exodus 2:24, 3:6, 2Kings 13:23) He talks to you about your children and your children's children. (Psalm 103:17,

Psalm 128:6) The blessings go down through a thousand generations. (Deuteronomy 7:9) He exhorts children to honor their mothers and fathers. (Deuteronomy 5:16) Legacy is part of God's plan for people to display His glory. But because you are not insulated from sin, the sins of the fathers are passed on to the sons (children) to the third and fourth generation. (Deuteronomy 5:9, Numbers 14:18) It is this sinful nature that blocks the release of the blessings for a thousand generations.

Mom and Dad: the First Line of Action

The most immediate generational sin is between parents and children. "He will turn the hearts of the parents to their children, and the hearts of the children to their parents." (Malachi 4:6) The Lord wants to reconcile the hearts of the parents to their children so that the children can go on to fulfill the destiny God planned for them. Parents and children against each other at any age will keep them from reaching God's best. Parents and children, beware!

The fifth commandment among the Ten Commandments is the only one with a consequence attached. (Exodus 20:12, Deuteronomy 5:16) "Honor your father and mother as the Lord has commanded you so that *YOU* may live long and that it may go well with *YOU* in the land that the

Lord God is giving *YOU*." (emphasis mine) Honoring your parents is not for their sake but your sake. Your relationship with your parents is crucial to your well- being. When you honor your parents, you are honoring God because He chose them for you (like it or not.)

God provided four things for Adam and Eve—bonding, boundaries, blessings, and dominion. We know God bonded with Adam and Eve because they had evening walks in the garden. He set a boundary when He told them not to eat of the tree of knowledge of good and evil. The tree itself was not bad. It was the object of obedience to God's command that was being tested. (Genesis 2:15) God blessed them by giving them everything in the garden and then gave them dominion over everything. (Genesis 1:27-30) The garden grew at God's hand. They just had to oversee it and enjoy the fruit and beauty.

To the extent that your parents follow God's model of providing the four elements of bonding, boundaries, blessings, and dominion in God's way, they are fulfilling what God intended. However, it's difficult to be human parents! They fail at times and sin against their children. If your parents were abusive, then you will have difficulty honoring them without discounting yourself. It is erroneous to believe that honoring father and mother means to be solicitous to them under a slave mentality, accepting abuse. Choosing to forgive them their sin against you, is honoring them. After clearing the spiritual path of sin, *you* will be changed. The best result would be to be reconciled with them, carrying no baggage from the past. In practical terms for cases of extreme abuse, it might mean limiting contact or learning to extricate yourself from situations of judgment or anger. At the very least, you could develop dispassionate respect.

If you fought with your parents as a young child or rebelled as a teenager, but now have a decent relationship, don't be fooled into thinking all is well. If you have never repented of the sin against your parents or never forgave them of the sin against you, the consequences will come in other ways. Your children may rebel against you or you may suffer from depression and joylessness. Unconfessed sin festers underground only to surface later in unexplainable discord. Repentance and forgiveness are keys to being set free from the effects of past sin. Honor your father and mother in this way so that all will go well with *you*.

No matter how good your relationship is now with your father and mother, if there was sin in the past that has never been confessed and repented, do it now and be free.

Some examples of children's sin against their parents:

- Sneaked out to parties when forbidden. (rebel against authority)

Blessings For a Thousand Generations

- Mumbled and grumbled over chores (Rebellious)
- Picked a fight with my siblings to distract the parents
- Ran away from home
- Disrespected my parents by cussing
- Physically violent with any parent
- Blame them for my bad choices

Some examples of what children need to forgive their parents for:

- berating me, lying to me
- embarrassing me in public
- keeping me from school causing me to fail
- incest and not protecting me from molestation
- leaving me home alone in charge of younger siblings
- making me take care of you when you were drunk or under drugs

Satan was cast out of heaven because he rebelled against God. If you rebelled, you too will be separated from God's best for you. If you were forced to do something illegal or immoral, admit it before God just the same so that it cannot be used against you. Remember, because you also live by perception and not only by fact, the perceived offense also must be forgiven. If you perceived that your dad hated you, forgive him even if you can't prove it. No amount of self-consolation will remove the pain. Forgive.

Below is a worksheet for you to use to remove ties of sin with your father and mother. The suggestions at the bottom are promptings. Not all will apply to you. Use one or two words to fill in the columns with the real and perceived sin(s) of your father and mother against you. Then fill the column of your sin(s) against them.

1. Be specific.
2. If the Lord gives you a remembrance, confess it.
3. Don't leave out anything you KNOW.
4. You don't have to be emotional, but you do need to be HONEST.

If you are doing this as a group prayer session, each person is to fill out a personal form. The leader will lead the participants to repeat the prayer. At the point where the details are to be spoken, let each person quietly whisper the sins. It should be spoken out loud enough for them to hear themselves. Do not "just think about it." Put a voice to it so that it is confessed. The leader then prompts the group to the conclusion of the prayer.

Worksheet for reconciling with your father.

Forgive father for:	Repent of: sins against father
I forgive my father for these and others I do not know or remember.	For these and other sins against my father I do not know or remember, I repent.

Forgive Father for:		Repent of sins against Father	
Abuse	Alcohol	Anger	Deceiving
Deception	Critical	Bitterness	Destruction
Indifference	Curfews	Despised	Drinking
Injustice	Disrespect	Disobedience	Fighting
Molestation	Drugs	Hatred	Hurting
Neglect	Ignorance	Judgment	Lying
Non-protecting	Poverty	Lying	Sabotage
	Restrictions	Rebellion	Smartmouth
Not Present	Rudeness	Resentment	Attacking

From your worksheet, pray the same prayers over your list "forgive father for."

"I forgive my father for (_read your list and line out each one_)."

For these and any other sins against me, known or unknown, intentional or unintentional, I forgive him. He does not have to make it up to me. He does not have to apologize. He does not have to give me reasons for his actions. He does not have to explain anything. He does not have to give me excuses. I release him 100%."

Pray this over the "Repent of sins against father" column, crossing out each item as you read your list.

"I repent of my sin against my father, especially (_read your list and line out_)."

(Pause) For any other sins, I do not know, or I cannot now remember, I repent. I also choose to forgive myself for my sin against my father."

Declare "It is finished."

Blessings For a Thousand Generations

Worksheet for reconciling with your mother

Forgive mother for:	Repent of sins against mother
I forgive my mother for these and other sins I do not know or remember.	For these and other sins of mine against my mother I do not know, or remember, I repent.

Repent of sins against mother		Forgive mother for:	
Attacking Complaining Disobedience Disrespectful Fake behavior Murmuring Rudeness Silence Skip school	Arguing Back Talk Betraying Criticize Cussing Discredit Ignoring Lying Mocking	Complaining Criticizing Demands Embarrass me Lying No guidance Not there Pressure Unaccepting	Abandonment Abuse Betrayal Cruel words Illness Restrictions Self –absorbed Too busy Unloving

From your worksheet, pray the same prayers over your list "forgive mother for."

"I forgive my mother for (_read your list and line out_). (Pause)

For these and any other sins against me, known or unknown, intentional or unintentional, I forgive her. She does not have to make it up to me. She does not have to apologize. She does not have to give me reasons for her actions. She does not have to explain anything. She does not have to give me excuses. I release her 100%."

Pray this over the "Repent of sins against mother" column, crossing out each item as you read your list.

"I repent of my sin against my Mother, especially (_read your list and line out_). (Pause) For any others, I do not know, or I cannot now remember, I repent. I also choose to forgive myself for my sin against my mother."

Forgive first, then repent. When you are finished and have crossed out everything on the list, declare, "It is finished."

PRAYER: "Lord, I have honored my father and mother as you have commanded by repenting and forgiving the sin between us. Thank you, Lord, for forgiving me and setting me free from ties of sin with my father and mother. I receive your generational blessings that are being released to me."

Don't Let History Repeat

The town of Flint, Michigan, had a source of pure water from the Detroit River. For budget concerns, the city council changed the source to the Flint River in 2014. The high lead content in the water was not treated properly, causing corrosion in the old lead pipes. People suffered from lead poisoning for two years by this water. When the problem was revealed in 2016, the water source was changed back to the Detroit River as its source. The now clean water continued to be contaminated because it flowed through the corroded pipes. To transport clean water, all source pipes and home pipes need to be replaced before the water will truly be lead-free.

God was Adam and Eve's source of pure life. They were convinced, by the devil, it was to their advantage to know good and evil so they ate of the tree God told them not to touch. Once they opened the generational line to sin, the following generations received contaminated life. To restore pure life, the lines must be replaced and the pure source re-established. To renew corroded generational lines is very expensive and extensive. It took obedience to pay for lives corroded by disobedience. Obedience costs everything. Jesus came to be the conduit back to the pure source of life with God. Jesus was obedient to the cross for the joy that the pipes to every individual will be cleansed and routed back to the Father. (Hebrews 12:2) When you make Jesus your Lord and Savior, you switch to the pure life source so the contaminated genealogical line can be purified to deliver pure life.

The only way unconfessed sin can be removed from the earth is through repentance and forgiveness under the blood of Jesus Christ. Excusing sin does not remove it. Such protestations as "I didn't know," "He made me do it," "I didn't know what else to do," are excuses. If you take something from a store without paying for it, you are stealing. It does not matter whether you did it on purpose, weren't paying attention when you walked out, or you needed it. It is still stealing. Only repentance and forgiveness remove sin and the consequences.

God looked for someone to stand in the gap but found no one so he provided Jesus (Isaiah 59: 16). We are the body of Christ therefore, with Christ living in us. We can stand in the gap to repent and forgive on behalf of our generations past. It is an honor and privilege to do the work of reconciliation on the earth through Christ in us. If you don't do it, the sin will be multiplied to the next generation. Everyone in succeeding generations will suffer until somebody steps into the gap. This kind of prayer is not a salvation prayer for past generations, nor is it a "taking the blame" for past generations. This type of prayer is designed to supernaturally replace contaminated pipes to release pure life to future generations.

Blessings For a Thousand Generations

The punishment of the sins of the fathers goes to the children to the third and fourth generations. (Deuteronomy 5:9, Numbers 14:18) The devil will try to continue the sin that was on a generation on through the next generation. This has been going on for years before you were born. The devil works through history to foment fear to kill, steal, and destroy anything God loves, especially you. War brings hatred, grief, and death. Tyranny produces destruction, widows, and orphans. Plagues bring disease, sickness, and disabilities. In economic disasters, people become refugees, homeless, and poor. The devil does not play fair. Fortunately for us, Jesus holds the redemption card. If we repent and forgive of any sin at the cross, the devil cannot hold it against us. It is absolved before God.

How History Impacted My Family:

The impact of World War II on Hawaii was greater in ways other parts of the country did not experience. I was born in Honolulu in 1945 at the end of the war in the Pacific Theater. On December 6, my dad worked the graveyard shift at Pearl Harbor Navy Shipyard. Fortunately, on December 7, 1941, he left the base at 5 a.m. after his shift. The Japanese bombing of Pearl Harbor happened at 8 a.m. There was heightened anxiety in the family in the ensuing days as they experienced "blackouts," air raids, and rationing. My parents were also Depression-Era people hoping to start a family. Money was scarce. They learned to "stretch the dollar until it squeaked." We were poor but not destitute. We wore "hand me downs," Mom cooked cheap meals, and we always made everything last as long as possible. There was nothing disposable. We saved string, rubber bands, newspapers, paper bags, milk cartons, jars, safety pins, and even wrapping paper. With his brothers, Dad built our two-car garage size house with his own hands.

My maternal grandparents were Chinese immigrants. Little did I know that long before the Pearl Harbor attack, war with Japan was going on in China, therefore, my grandfather loathed everything Japanese—food, clothing, people, and art. Racism surfaced when my grandparents believed their greatest achievement was that each of their eight children married Chinese spouses. My surviving grandmother was very wary, and my parents were cautious when I married a Caucasian man. Their world was shaken when we adopted a Vietnamese son and a Korean daughter. I was compelled to repent and forgive all sin of prejudice brought on by history on behalf of my generation's past. Since then we have enjoyed an abundant life of an international family and multi-cultural living. The blessings flow. God says the blessings will go to a thousand generations.

Below is a worksheet to help you discover any historical generational sins that impact you and your family that need to be forgiven so that the blessings can flow.

Worksheet for Generational History

What is your ancestry? _____

How many generations of family stories can you remember? _____

Were any of your ancestors refugees or immigrants? Describe, as well as you can, their experiences.

If your parents, or grandparents, or even you entered any country illegally, repent of law-breaking so the blessings they sought can flow to them and you. Describe the situation.

Tell what you know about any family members who experienced war.

Did any family members live under ethnic persecution? Why were they persecuted?

Were any of your ancestors <u>*persecutors*</u>? Explain the situation as you know it.

Blessings For a Thousand Generations

The promise to Abraham is that anyone who blessed him (his line) will be blessed and any who cursed him (his line) will be cursed. (Genesis 12:3) Did any group of your ancestral line persecute Jews? When did this happen?

Were there any traitors of among ancestors? If so, explain.

How has your personal history been impacted by world history?

If you are doing this in group prayer, share what was revealed to you.

Here are prayers of repentance and forgiveness addressing historical generational sin.

- Lord, I admit that my ancestral line suffered (_poverty, orphaned, murder, exclusion, slavery, etc ..._)

- On behalf of myself and my ancestors past, to Adam before the fall, I repent of these historical sins: (_bigotry, hatred, murder, cruelty, greed, deceit, illegal immigration jealousy, etc ..._)

- On behalf of myself and my ancestors past, to Adam before the fall, I forgive those who sinned against us historically through (_persecution, slavery, atrocities, robbery, etc. ..._)

- Lord, I admit and confess these sins of my generations past.

- On behalf of my generations to the 3rd and 4th generation, back to Adam before the fall, I repent of these sins and any others that I do not know which block your blessings.

- On behalf of my generations past, all the way back to Adam before the fall, I forgive all those persons, institutions, and situations that sinned against us.

Blessings For a Thousand Generations

- I now release them. They owe us nothing--no restitution, no apology, no reasons, no explanations, and no excuses. I release them 100%.

- I declare the bondages of historical sins of my ancestors and family line are now broken.

- AMEN

Impact of Infirmity

Our physical bodies are vessels appointed to carry the presence of God into the world. Infirmities last a long time, causing weakness in body and mind. Conditions as diabetes, Parkinson's, and migraines are infirmities. The devil will attack your physical body to weaken and disable you, stirring your anger toward God.

God said, (Exodus 15:26) "If you listen carefully to the Lord your God and do what is right in his eyes, if you pay attention to his commands and keep all his decrees, I will not bring on you any of the **diseas**es I brought on the Egyptians, for I am the Lord, who heals you." There was disobedience somewhere in past generations. The devil does not care whether disobedience was by ignorance or by intention. He will lead you as far away from God as you are willing to go. He will trick you into doing and saying things without thinking. He knows the power of the tongue, so he will goad you into doing his dirty work for him through your mouth.

Examples of speaking infirmity against yourself:

- I'm sick and tired of....
- You will be the death of me...
- If that happens again, I'll die.
- I'll kill myself if you...

- I hate myself.
- I am so ugly, clumsy, ditzy, forgetful, . . .

God will forgive you and shut the door to the devil any and every time you repent and forgive. God does not keep score. However, you must repent to a deep level to be free from the devil's clutches. God will give you supernatural strength to stay the course to make changes so you won't have to endlessly repent.

Worksheet for Generational Infirmities

What infirmities are attached to you?

What infirmities are in your family now and in generations past?

Examples:
Cancer
Alzheimer's
Kidney Failure
Parkinson's
Heart Disease
Colitis
Diabetes
Allergies
Acne
Arthritis
Chrohn's Disease
Chronic Fatigue
Dyslexia
Epilepsy
Fibromyalgia
Lukemia
Sciatica

High Blood Pressure
Multiple Sclerosis
Lupus
Ulcers
Autoimmunine dysfunction
Sleep Apnea
Weight Problems

Ask the Holy Spirit for a revelation of where the infirmity entered.

Lord, where did these diseases enter my bloodline? (example: Grandfather was a very bitter man)

Lord, how did these diseases enter my bloodline? (example: alcohol, drugs, uncontrolled eating)

Of what do I need to repent?

Of what and whom do I need to forgive?

Somewhere in your generation line, the door was opened to infirmity. Someone could have been the initiator of sin or a victim of sin. The devil does not care how the door was opened, just that it is open. Name that the infirmity so it can be brought into the light of Christ. If you deny its existence, it will have the right to stay.

Repent: "I admit these infirmities are in my family line (__diabetes, a heart condition, gout, cancer, Parkinson's etc . . .__), "I repent of any sin in the family that opened the door to these infirmities.

Forgive: "I forgive members of my family line for accepting these diseases through invitation, poor health habits, or not caring for their bodies."

"I close the door to (__list__)"

"I declare that my bloodline is now cleansed of all infirmity because of Jesus' shed blood. In the name of Jesus, I break the bondage of this infirmity in my bloodline. I declare infirmity is removed from me and my generations forward."

Trails of Iniquity (Isaiah 59: 2)

Sin is anything that does not glorify God and is out of alignment with his Word. When sin is repetitive it becomes an iniquity. A college student who gets drunk at a birthday party would be in sin. If he chooses drunkenness every weekend and becomes addicted to alcohol, he has invited an iniquity in his bloodline. Iniquities of betrayal, lying, physical abuse, and even anger can attach to a bloodline. An iniquity usually is set in motion by a repeated choice for sin. The iniquity attached to the DNA passes on to the next generation. Just as sin can be removed through repentance and forgiveness, iniquity can also be removed when confessed on behalf of generations past cleansing the bloodline.

A woman "Sally" told me she was worried her daughter would become pregnant before marriage. According to her family history, she bore a child before marriage, her mother had a child before marriage, and her mother was the child of grandmother's pre-marriage romance. Although Sally married her child's father, she knew her premarital pregnancy was out of line with God. Bearing children outside of the marriage covenant had set the bastard spirit in the family line keep them in bondage to inferiority and rejection spirits.

Covenant-breaking in divorce becomes an iniquity when the grandparents, parents, and adult children are all divorced, perhaps more than once. Child abuse becomes an iniquity when the abused become abusers. What might have started as a discipline, turned into physical, mental, or emotional abuse. Other iniquities include abortion, alcoholism, adultery, or rage. These sins can be repented and forgiven to supernaturally break the bondage of iniquity.

Worksheet on Generational Iniquity

Identify any iniquities that may be in your family line. List the ones you do know then ask the Holy Spirit to reveal what you don't know that needs to be confessed.

Read this prayer, filling in the blanks.

"On behalf of myself and my generations past and future, I repent of:

- The iniquity (iniquities) of _____

- I repent of making these iniquities an idol in my life.

- I forgive those who tempted my ancestors into iniquities.

Blessings For a Thousand Generations

- I forgive those who tempted my generations into iniquities.

- I forgive all situations that aided and abetted iniquity in our bloodline.

- I release them totally . . . no restitution, no apology, no reason, no explanation, no excuses

- I declare that my bloodline is now cleansed by the Blood of Jesus.

Declare this:

- "I release the blessings of the Lord for a thousand generations from Adam before the fall, and all generations forward through eternity."

- "I release heath, wealth, prosperity, possession of lands, family reconciliation, salvation, freedom, healthy marriages, healthy children, wisdom, intimacy with Christ, and obedience to God."

Put your hands on yourself. Declare: "In Jesus' name I release the supernatural blessings of the Lord to a thousand generations."

Chapter 4
Is Sin Crouching At Your Door?
(Genesis 5:7)

Keep the Doors Shut

Repentance and forgiveness will be applied to five doorways of sin. Charts are provided for each section. Use the charts as a guide for both visual, writing, and speaking the prayers. If this is for a group, each member can create a similar chart as the exercise proceeds.

Innocent Bloodshed

This is not about war or about a judgment that was imposed by a court of law. This is about individuals who take out their rage, frustrations, ungodly passions, and revenge on others.

God values life. The first incident of innocent bloodshed was Cain killing Abel because Abel's sacrifice was received by God and his not. (Genesis 4:4-9) Herod, driven by fear of being usurped, ordered the baby boys in Bethlehem under the age of two murdered because he wanted to kill the young King of the Jews. (Matthew 2:16) Haman plotted to have all the Jews killed during the time of Esther because the Agagites hated the Jews. (Esther 3:6) Drive-by shootings, mall massacres, hit-and-run driving, and abortion all fall in the category of innocent bloodshed. Any kind of revenge, payback, or murder is taking judgment into your own hands. God executes judgment through the court of law. Physical, emotional, or mental abuse is innocent bloodshed. When people are abusing each other, they are under the sin of innocent bloodshed and have lined up with the devil.

My story:

I am a diminutive person, less than five feet tall and under a hundred pounds dripping wet. My mother told me that when I was a toddler, all the other kids my age were about twice my size. When they pushed me around, as children will, I fought back by biting their arms. I had a fierce spirit and a loud voice, so I would fend for myself by being the boss.

Is Sin Crouching At Your Door? (Genesis 5:7)

Years later, in a graduate class of about twenty students, the students were asked to introduce themselves giving name, hometown, and why they were in this course. I had no fear of speaking in public, but, when my turn came, I was suddenly tongue-tied. I could not remember my name, hometown, nor why I was there. After gentle prompting by the instructor, I managed to blurt out something that might have made sense.

That evening, as I was doing the homework, I became puzzled over that scene. It did not make any sense to me, as I was an experienced speaker. I had taught at the college level and had even conducted a 150-person chorus and orchestra.

"Holy Spirit what was that all about in class? What kept me from just giving my name, city, and why I am here?"

"The spirit of intimidation lurks."

The Holy Spirit revealed that the spirit of intimidation had attached to me, and it would do its paralyzing work when I least expected it. To get free of this attachment, I was to repent and forgive. First, I forgave all the people who had intimidated me in the past. I forgave grandparents and teachers, dates and bosses, even waiters in restaurants. I then repented of all the times that I had intimidated others, including my cousins, my children, students, and even service personnel in my home. Then I repented of holding resentment in my heart when intimidated by others. By repenting and forgiving, I removed any sin that gave intimidation any right to operate in my life. I was set free from even perceiving that I was being intimidated. I received new confidence. To this day, when intimidation tries to grip me, I can ward off the attack. Intimidation is a form of innocent bloodshed that causes you, in turn, to intimidate others.

Prayer Exercise:

Repent: Make a list of those whom you abused at any time in your life. Include behaviors in which you bullied anyone (for example, making your sister cry); when you used rage to control others; if you called others names to their faces or behind their backs; when you played pranks that put others to shame; or if you used obscenities against anyone. You may have thought that you were just expressing your frustration, when in fact, you were opening doors for innocent bloodshed in the form of intimidation.

My sin of innocent bloodshed.

_____
_____
_____

Is Sin Crouching At Your Door? (Genesis 5:7)

Pray this: "Lord, I repent of my sin of innocent bloodshed especially. . . (read your list). As I repent and forgive, you are merciful and just to forgive me. Thank you for closing the door of the sin of innocent bloodshed in my life."

Forgive: Make a list of people who have abused you in any way. Forgive anyone or anything that abused you, or that you perceive abused you, *at any time in your life*. Include teachers, coaches, parents, grandparents, relatives, neighbors, other students, bosses, and anybody who harmed or offended you. Remember, you live by perception, so if you *believe* someone abused you, add them to your list. This is not the time to analyze whether or not they abused you.

Sin of abuse against me.

_____
_____
_____

Pray this: "Lord I forgive. . . . (read your list) for abusing me in the past. They owe me nothing: no restitution, no apology, no reasons, no explanation, and no excuses. I release them 100%."

You may think this did not affect you if you have not suffered any major consequences. On the other hand, you do not know what blessings you missed, or were blocked from you. If you continue to abuse others or support others to be abusive, you will re-open the door to innocent bloodshed to invade your life. Don't let it in. Be vigilant. Keep repenting and forgiving until you are set free. If you continue to be abused, get yourself out of harm's way as best you can. Keep your heart clean so the Lord can supernaturally move on your behalf.

Sexual Sin

Without a body, you would not be able to function in the world. Sexual sins are sins against the body, either yours or someone else's. God wants to show his glory through your body so it's important to keep it clean and holy. The body is the temple of the Holy Spirit. Sexual intimacy between husband and wife under covenant with each other is holy, as God intended. Sexual activity of a married person, outside of the covenant, is adultery. Sexual activity between non-married persons is fornication. (1Corinthians 6:18, Romans 7:3)

The consequences of sexual sin found in the Bible are dire. Samson was a handsome, strong, important leader in Israel for twenty years but He could not control his

Is Sin Crouching At Your Door? (Genesis 5:7)

passions. (Judges 15:20) There were many beautiful women in Israel, but he was attracted to the Philistine women, Israel's enemy. He abandoned his first Philistine wife causing great strife. Delilah, his second attraction, brought his downfall as she lured him to divulge the secret of his great strength. God may have had other plans for Samson to accomplish his destiny, but Samson's bad choices made him powerless. After years of hard labor and humiliation, God still allowed him to destroy Israel's enemy, the Philistines (Judges 14- 16). David was a powerful king but he too could not control his passions. His sin with Bathsheba was compounded by arranging Uriah's murder on the front lines of battle. The prophet Nathan unveiled David's sin. Although David repented, the price was the death of the son that was conceived. (2Samuel 11). The children of Israel were lured into idolatry through sexual sin while encamped in Shittim. They were ready to enter the Promised Land! Balaam could not curse them so he lured them into sexual sin. (Numbers 25:1-3, Revelation 2:14) Sexual sin separates you from God.

Though tempted by Potiphar's wife, Joseph was able to resist her and kept himself pure. He spent time in jail for resisting her temptations, but he remained true to God. As he was faithful to God, he was groomed for promotion. He practiced his gift of dream interpretation in the prison. He was gracious to the cupbearer who would later bring him before Pharaoh. Joseph was released from jail, not because he was innocent but because he was faithful to God. Supernatural promotion awaited him. (Genesis 39:6-10)

When sex is perverted, trouble begins. Sexuality is God's gift to you for the physical enjoyment of covenant union between husband and wife and for procreation of godly children. Married people are still under covenant without bearing children.

(1Corinthians 6:12-20) You were created to be in union with only one partner. Sexual intimacy builds soul ties between partners. (1Corinthians 6:15) Marriage requires a dedicated connection. "Forsaking all others" means to have a dedicated soul tie keeping faith with only your marriage partner.

It is important to break soul ties with former partners and spouses whether divorced or widowed. Pre-marital sexual sin creates soul ties outside of the marriage covenant. Multiple soul ties put confusion in the soul. Illegal soul ties must be broken to restore purity. Sexual union outside the covenant of marriage is sin. Consensual sexual sin means that the parties have willingly opened the doors to sin. It does not negate the fact it is sin.

Sexual slurs and innuendos contaminate your thoughts and speech. Molestation and rape against you or by you are the most damaging of sexual sins. The combination of violence against an innocent one through sexual sin fractures the soul and defiles the body. Pornography, printed or online, is virtual sexual engagement with a non-spouse. Sexual aberrations such as sodomy, incest, or prostitution all violate the sanctity of the body.

Both men and women are tempted with sexual sins. Temptation is all around in billboards, language, movies, and music. These same temptations push you to the entertainment phase of sin. When sex is flaunted as desirable entertainment, the time between thought and commitment is short-circuited into moments. Sexual sin is often shrouded in secrecy bringing shame. Shame will keep you in hiding. (1Peter 2:11) Rather than accepting sexual sin as the norm, run from it and pursue the right motives and right living. (2Timothy 2:22)

Athena's Story

"Athena" told me she felt men were always leering at her wherever she went. She was married and has remained faithful to her husband, but is frequently accused of "playing around". She revealed that, as a teenager, she had lived a promiscuous life with many casual partners and one serious boyfriend. At the time, she knew that this lifestyle was wrong, but enjoyed being the center of attention. When she married, she decided to be faithful to her husband. Because she never repented of the past sexual sins and never cut the illegal soul ties created with multiple partners, the sinful assignment of sexual promiscuity remained attached to her. The shame and lewdness of the past followed her around. When she repented and forgave those who engaged with her and forgave herself, she could cut the ungodly soul ties that were formed. By being cleansed, she was set free from past soul ties and could now be restored to purity with her husband.

Prayer Exercise: List the partners, if you can. The more specific you are, the deeper the forgiveness will be. This is to remove shame, not hide it.

Partners in sexual sin

_____
_____
_____

"Lord, I repent for engaging in illegal sexual activity especially with (_list_)

Sexual sin against me

_____
_____
_____

Prayer:

I forgive those who engaged with me, lured me, and tempted me in sexual sin. They owe me nothing—no restitution, no apology, no reasons, no explanations, no excuses. I now release them 100%.

I forgive myself for engaging in illegal sexual sin. I do not have to make up for it, no apology, no reasons, no explanations, and no excuses are due me. I release myself 100%.

As I have repented and forgiven, you are merciful and just to forgive me. By faith, through Jesus Christ, I accept my forgiveness. I am now cleansed by the blood of Jesus and break the bonds of soul ties and uncleanness. I reclaim my sexual purity."

Covenant Breaking

Contracts are based on delivery. In a sales contract, if you do not pay for the goods, the supplier is not obligated to deliver. Conversely, if they do not deliver, you do not have to pay.

Covenants, however, are deeper. God is very serious about covenants. Covenant agreements are made between two parties involving a vow and some kind of symbol or seal. The agreement lasts a lifetime, only released by death. God promises to be your God, provider, and protector. You promise to worship Him and have no other gods. Regardless of your faithfulness to worship and honor Him, God always keeps his part of the covenant. Even if you think you have given him good reason to break the covenant, He never will.

God made a covenant with Abraham and sealed it with fire over animal sacrifice. He said, "I will make you the father of many nations. I will bless those who bless you, and curse those who curse you." (Genesis 12:3) God made a covenant with Noah and sealed it with a rainbow promising never to destroy mankind through catastrophic flood ever again. (Genesis 9:16) God made a covenant with the Jews through Moses to be their God and be whoever they needed him to be, the great I AM. (Exodus 14:14-15) Jacob made a covenant to serve God in exchange for provision. (Genesis 28:20) David made a covenant with Jonathan over Jonathan's descendants. (1Samuel 20:41-42) David looked after Meshiboeth after Jonathan's death. Joshua made a covenant with the Gibeonites that they would not be attacked or wiped out from the earth. (Joshua 9:14-18) Saul violated the covenant made on behalf of the Israelites and his descendants paid with their lives. (2 Samuel 21:1-9) God made a covenant with mankind to send a Savior whose blood would forgive sins through eternity to bring them into their destiny. (Luke 1:67-75) Jesus Christ was the sacrifice that sealed the agreement.

Is Sin Crouching At Your Door? (Genesis 5:7)

In the covenant of marriage, the man and woman promise to love, honor, and cherish each other until death parts them. Marriage vows are sealed with the giving of rings. The parties promise to keep their part of the agreement until death, regardless of circumstances. It is not "until we don't like each other anymore" or "until we agree to divorce". Former marriage partners can still love, honor, and cherish each other after divorce, even if they are not living together, or being intimate partners. Sometimes, honoring means staying away, so that they do not continue to sin with harassment and bickering. Loving means not judging, criticizing, or holding hatred in the heart. Cherish means seeing each other as someone precious to the Lord.

When you make a covenant at baptism to follow Jesus for life, it does not mean you will never make mistakes or stray. It means that Jesus will continue to play an important part in your life. You cannot "divorce" Jesus. The Christian's covenant as God's adopted child is never broken. When you have children, there is a covenant to nourish, protect, and guide them into godly adulthood. Your children, whether biologically born to you or adopted, will always be your children.

Broken promises lead the way to broken covenants. Carelessness in keeping promises in things such as doing what you say you are going to do, being on time, or keeping business commitments, pave the way to covenant-breaking. If you consistently break promises, you will have difficulty grasping God's covenant with you. He is a promise-keeping God.

Exercise Concerning Broken Covenants

List any covenants broken in your life--marriage, parental, baptismal, broken promises. Covenants broken by you or against you are equally damaging. List the broken covenants or promises in your life.

Covenants I have broken.

_____
_____
_____

Prayer

Lord, I repent of breaking covenant with (__name__) in (__marriage, parenting, etc.__) (Be specific. Repeat as necessary)

I repent of breaking promises I have made to(my children, bosses, family. Be specific.)

Is Sin Crouching At Your Door? (Genesis 5:7)

Covenants that others have broken with me.

_____
_____
_____

I now choose to forgive those who have broken covenant with me, especially _____.

I forgive those who have broken promises with me. They owe me nothing: no restitution, no apology, no reasons, no explanation, and no excuses. I release them 100%."

I forgive myself for breaking covenants and promises with   God, my spouse, my children, etc.

Thank you, Lord, that as I choose to repent and forgive, you supernaturally forgive me. I now close the door on broken covenants in my life and seal it with the name of Jesus.

Idolatry

God is a jealous God. He does not want any other god to have your affections or worship because God knows He cannot pour his best into you if you give the credit to another god. He wants you and the world to know that all good gifts come from Him. As you give Him the credit, He can pour out more and more on your behalf. Worshiping other gods diminishes you, not God.

The Israelites were to always worship God but when they entered the Promised Land, they made covenants with the gods of the Canaanites. God promised that he would never break his covenant with them, even when they broke covenant with Him. He never left them. He let them wander in the wilderness until they came to their senses. He tested their loyalty. They needed to know how to war to possess the new land as their assignment was to rid their Promised Land of the idol worship. (Judges 2:1-5) They instead incorporated idol worship. God still kept his part of the covenant by allowing the next generation to enter the Promised Land.

There are godly covenants and wicked covenants. Godly covenants have a Biblical basis and bring glory to God. Individuals or groups can make a covenant with Satan, Allah, Masons, or cartels and mafia. No matter how enticingly disguised, wicked covenants operate in the supernatural to glorify the devil. They grip life unto death. You will want to be careful not to engage in them. You cannot serve God and idols. To the extent that you worship anything else, you decrease your connection with God. If you have ever participated in the worship of another god of another religion, repent today and close the door of idol worship.

Is Sin Crouching At Your Door? (Genesis 5:7)

. . .

My Story

I was not born into a Christian family. My grandparents and parents practiced a combination of Chinese ancestral worship, Buddhism, and Taoism. My maternal grandmother consulted the Buddhist priests about wedding dates, children's names, and future spouses for her children. Each year, she set up an altar and worshipped something at the full moon and Chinese New Year. That was a Chinese tradition full of celebration, food, fun, and family time.

In elementary school, a friend invited me to Sunday school. It was fun because it was something special to do on Sunday. I made friends and was attracted to prayer as I learned about Jesus., As I entered the seventh grade, my parents, seeking high academic standards, enrolled me in St. Andrew's Priory, an Episcopal School for girls. There I learned what it meant to be a follower of Jesus. I thought I was already following him because I went to church. Most of the girls at the school were Christians from Christian families who attended church. Religious education classes awakened my spirit to things I had never known before. By the eighth grade, I wanted to make my commitment to Jesus.

In the Chinese tradition, it is customary to acknowledge dead ancestors with ritual offerings of food, incense, and folded paper money and clothing until their 100th birthday. My mother carried on this tradition for my paternal grandfather, who had died when he was 35. She explained that it was her duty as the wife of the oldest son to honor her deceased father-in-law. I helped her prepare and do the rituals. Eventually, I came to realize that some of this was idol worship. As a new Christian, I wondered whether I should now be participating in that *ancestral* ritual at all. I was conflicted. My priest, being well versed in the local traditions, advised me to continue honoring my parents in this way as long as they requested. When they no longer asked, I would be free to walk away from it. While away at college, I did not carry on those religious traditions.

In the Bible, after Naaman was healed, he promised to worship the God of Israel but asked for forgiveness for what he had done and was required to do while serving his master in the worship of other gods. (2Kings 5:17b-19) As I learned more about idolatry, I repented of unintentional idol worship because of ignorance. The Lord's forgiveness set me free.

Besides idols from other religions or traditions, invisible idols can form. The formation starts with a thought such as "I'm not very smart." This might have been spoken to you through classmates, teachers, or family or even yourself to get out of some assignment. This becomes the pedestal of the idol. Without realizing it, you collect evidence to prove the statement is true and it takes on a life of its own. Idols need evidence that it should direct your life. The more evidence you collect, the more it will demand of you. You will even set yourself up for failure so that you can prove the belief that "I'm not very smart" is true. Although there may be more evidence to the contrary, you will not be able to see it.

The **idol of self** constantly collects evidence based on the lies of "I have to do things myself," or "I have no one to help me." You may have received help in various ways such as personal contacts, teams of assistance, the task reduced, or even angels, but you will fail to see them. You forget that the Holy Spirit is your Helper and you are God's partner.

Chasing after **wealth** for wealth's sake makes you greedy and dissatisfied. The **wealth idol** will amplify your lack rather than your blessing. You will harbor a poverty mentality no matter how big your bank account. You might even squander God's provision because the idol wants you to keep impoverished. Gratitude is shallow and you forget that God gives the *power* to get wealth. (Deuteronomy 8:18)

The **tolerance idol** has been renamed the "politically correct" idol. This one blurs the lines between good and evil, and acceptable and unacceptable behavior. It will cause you to step outside moral boundaries because you believe you must allow people to bully you, bend the rules, or cheat. You will fail to speak the truth in love. Your ethics are compromised for fear of being "intolerant." Forgiveness, not tolerance, is the Christian's watchword.

The **job or career idol** steals from your family, your health, your friendships, and your time. When you sacrifice everything and anything to satisfy the job, you are in trouble. A pastor once told me that one day he realized he was thinking as God's employee rather than God's partner. Working as God's partner would add to him not diminish him.

Relatives will become an idol if you spend all your energy satisfying what they think you ought to do. Aiding relatives out of love is one thing, but running to each one's beck and call to keep them happy violates your freedom.

When you are in idolatry, you are always looking for evidence to bolster the idol and prove that its lies are true. You can even make God an idol. If you find yourself always trying to make God happy rather than enjoying his presence, then you have made Him an idol. God as an idol *takes* from you. God as a Father *gives* to you. When you are in obedience to God, he gives you opportunities, self-confidence, boldness, and grace. You do not have to keep looking for ways to make Him happy. He wants to give you

Is Sin Crouching At Your Door? (Genesis 5:7)

His happiness.

When you worship God, you only need to stand in faith. He will never break his covenant with you. You do not need to prove to yourself and others that he is good. He may hide for a time so you will learn to seek Him. God did not remove all the enemies from the Promised Land because the Israelites needed to learn to lean on God to fight their battles. You will be tested with tasks to accomplish for your own sake. The small paycheck may remain until you learn to budget, learn to pay your debts, or give. The cranky boss may remain until you learn to forgive and not be cranky yourself. The bossy neighbor may remain until you learn to control your mouth. You are being taught by experience.

Prayer Exercise:

List any of the suggested idols or any others you see which control your life.

Idols I have created and worshipped.

_____
_____
_____

Idols that have been put into my life by others.

_____

_____

_____

Prayer

"Lord, I repent of worshipping any other god or trusting in another god at any time in my life. I repent of sharing my worship with other gods. I repent of opening my soul to other gods. I repent of creating other gods in my mind and soul, collecting evidence for their lies, especially those of (__list__).

I forgive those who have led me to worship other gods. I forgive myself for seeking other gods & religions. I forgive myself for creating idols to replace You or share Your throne in my heart. Amen."

Deception

Satan is called the Deceiver and the Father of Lies (John 8:44). Deception is a willful act to hide what is leading to betrayal and mistrust. If you engage in deceiving others, chances are good that you too will be deceived. Deception creeps into your life by making you think there is a benefit. Children deceive their parents or friends to gain an advantage. Those who use deception as a game or a prank do not realize they are opening the door to the deceptive spirit to continue to operate in their lives in the future. Deceptions like these will trip you up throughout life.

1. Using a fake ID card
2. Lying about your status in school
3. Lying about immigration status
4. Making idle promises that you have no intention of keeping
5. Say you will put God first, but give God your leftovers of time, energy, and money
6. Using dishonest practices in business. (Proverbs 11:1)
7. Not following through with integrity.

Prayer Exercise:

List deceptions you have perpetrated.

_____
_____
_____

"Lord I repent of deceiving others especially read your list ."

Have you been a victim of deception?

1. You were ripped off in a business deal
2. You were stood up on a date
3. A glowing job description turned out to be slavery
4. You were told you could advance in a company, but it never happened
5. Your insurance coverage had exclusions for almost everything
6. You were told there was "no obligation" but found you were obligated to buy

Deceptions against me

_____
_____
_____

Forgive

"Lord, I forgive those who have deceived me, especially __read your list__. They owe me nothing. They do not have to make it up to me with restitution. They owe me no apology, no reasons necessary, no explanations necessary, and no excuses. I release them 100%.

As I have repented and forgiven deeds of deception, I receive the forgiveness of sin by faith in Jesus Christ. I renounce deception and remove the veil of deception that was over my eyes.

When you are more interested in being reconciled than being right, it is easier to choose to repent and forgive. Being reconciled allows you to fully receive the blessings of God.

Watch Out for Air Attacks

About 20 years ago, I volunteered as an aid to doctors on a mission health clinic. We traveled in small single-engine planes that could land on a dirt road in the cornfields. There was no airport near our appointed village. Aid workers and rescue teams used this landing strip, and so did drug runners, smugglers, and fugitives. There was no control tower and no security monitoring of who came and went.

Unchecked, the devil will use landing strips paved with lies based on your life experiences. You will be deceived into thinking your defense mechanisms against future hurts or betrayals were built for a good reason. The landings will stop for a season but as long as the strip is still functional the devil will have access. When a lie is triggered, you will be bombarded with emotional and mental assaults.

Some common landing strips are:

1. *What others tell you about you* that are not in agreement with God. "You'll never succeed," "You're stupid," "You never get it right," "Nobody loves you."
2. *What you believe about yourself.* All of the above lies plus, "God is mad at me," "I have to do everything perfectly," "I can't afford to be wrong," "I won't succeed, so why bother trying?"
3. *Rationalizations for temptations.* "It's fun," "Nobody gets hurt," "It's just a joke," "Nobody cares anyway."
4. *The negative self-talk* that invites striving. "I have to look good," "No one will pay attention to me," "I need to hide," "Taking credit for something good is bragging."

You came into agreement with the above lies through life events. You even rationalize that God was trying to teach you something. God can teach you anything without cutting Himself off. He just needs you to agree with His Word so He can perform it. He is searching your heart for His Word so he can agree with you. You don't need to go around quoting Scripture like a talking Bible. Remember to do justly, love mercy, and walk humbly with God. (Micah 6:8) Think about what is lovely, just, of good report, and excellent. (Philippians 4:8) God is for you, not against you. He is not criticizing you, so you do not need to criticize yourself (Psalm 27:1-2) He wants you to trust Him. Keep your behavior and desires godly.

You can destroy the devil's landing strips by repenting for agreeing with the lies and acting on them. Forgive anyone and anything that put the lies there. Expose the circumstances that allowed the devil to build a landing strip by confessing them.

Prayer to destroy the devil's landing strips.

Anything that contradicts the Word and character of God is a lie. List the thoughts that keep you down and the events that trigger an explosion in you.

_____
_____
_____

Prayer:

I repent of allowing the devil to build with his lies landing strips in my life. Especially these I have listed. (Nobody wants me; everything I do fails; I'll never get it right; everybody is better than me, etc.)

I forgive myself for inviting the devil to build his landing strip in my life. I repent of not storing and obeying the Word of God in my heart. I choose to activate and obey the Word in my heart to dispel the lies. I choose to be vigilant in detecting future landings in my thoughts, words, and deeds. I invite You, Lord to destroy the landing strips that were built by the devil. Amen

After you pray this prayer or one similar to it that fits your situation, wait to sense what God will do for you. When I have prayed this prayer with others, some have seen an earthquake destroy the landing strip, seen a fire burn it up, or have it replaced with a meadow. All received a sense of peace. God does not need a landing strip built for him. He needs permission from you to share your life and dance with him. Invite him by praying, "Jesus, I invite you to enter my life and be my dance partner."

Chapter 5
Leave Mistakes Behind

All the foregoing exercises in this book were designed to increase the quality of your worship. If you ever wondered whether God listens to you, just worship Him. Worship gets God's attention like nothing else. Praise Him. Make the choice to exalt Him. Be his friend. Scripture says we become like the God we worship. (Psalm 115: 4-8) Jesus is the model that allows us to see and be like him.

True worship is in Spirit and in Truth. (John 4:24) Spirit because our spirit man is right with God through repentance and forgiveness. Truth is when we are transparent before God, hiding nothing. Worship is deeper than singing praise music, dancing, or shouting because others are doing it. Worship has substance.

Ask, Seek, and Knock

The Bible tells you to ask, seek, and knock, and it shall be opened to you. (Matthew. 7:7) Who should you ask? The most common answer is, God. But consider some practical aspects. If you want to attend college, you *ask* the college counselor about the requirements, the application, the cost, and the acceptance policy. You then research the colleges that will fulfill your desired course of study, your budget, and the location that's right for you. This *seeking* prepares you to receive the blessing you want. When you have all your materials and requirements ready, you then *knock* on the college door by submitting your application. If your application is incomplete, or your fee was not included, you may get no answer. There are practical things you need to do correctly. Likewise, God will provide the answers through the right sources.

Actions in the natural world reflect actions in the spiritual world when you pray "thy will be done on earth as it is in heaven." You must be ready to receive what you are asking for. Christians often ask for things but are not ready to receive them. You may not get that promotion because you are not ready for the added responsibility. Will wealth be used for more self- promotion? If your heart is harboring resentment and anger, your healed body will not bring glory to God. We are participants in the answers. (John

15:5-8) God will wait for you to be ready before He bestows His favor.

Chosen

God has everything prepared for you to succeed in the destiny he has planned for you. (Jeremiah 29:11-13). When you say, "Yes," in agreement with God, you are chosen. You have the final say. He will do all that is necessary for you to finish the course. You could say "No" to that path and destiny at any time and step outside His will. Hearing the call alone does not make you chosen. (1 Samuel 3:4-10) You must volunteer to be chosen. Sometimes circumstances and hardships seem to volunteer you, but they just make you eligible to be chosen. You have the right gift mix for success in God's plan for you. Don't despair if you are not chosen for something outside of your sphere. I admire athletes, but I know I was not chosen to be one of them.

I remember always being the last to be chosen on the basketball or volleyball team in high school physical education classes. Team captains wanted to put together a winning team. I was only 4'10" tall and mere 78 pounds with not much athletic ability. I was always chosen to be a scorekeeper or a linesman because that did not require height or athletic ability. I was discouraged to be overlooked but took heart on the academic scene where I was regularly chosen to be the team leader, the spokesman, or a committee chairman.

God didn't wonder who would bring Jesus into the world by searching for the eligible women. God prepared Mary for generations with the right lineage to be the mother of Jesus for the right time in history, betrothed to Joseph. Joseph was also chosen so that there would be an earthly father ready to receive God's son. Both said, "Yes," and were obedient to God's plan. Saul became the first king of Israel but he failed the tests of faithfulness and obedience. (1Samuel 15:12-23) Although David was not Saul's son, he was a forerunner of the Messiah. (Matthew 1:1-17). He was trained in the fields as a shepherd, for he would have to shepherd a nation. He was also trained as a warrior, for that moment in history when Israel needed a champion warrior. Whether shepherd, warrior, or king, David said, "Yes," to God, despite his weaknesses.

In the early 1860s, George Washington Carver's parents were slaves owned by Moses and Susan Carver in Missouri, USA. When George was just one year old, he and his mother were kidnapped, but only young George was later rescued. The Carvers then raised George as their child. In 1864, slavery was abolished, and while his birth parents had been slaves, George lived as a free man in the Carver household. The Carvers taught George to read and

Leave Mistakes Behind

write, and sent him to high school as George Carver. Colleges rejected him because of his race, so he established a homestead with a conservatory of plants and flowers. While studying art, his art instructor encouraged him to study botany. He soon became known as a botanist and inventor who promoted crops of peanuts and sweet potatoes as an alternative to cotton. He was placed in history at the right time with the ability to pursue such discoveries.

In July 1902, Willis Carrier invented the system of air cooling and humidity control for a New Jersey printing press, to stabilize the contracting and expanding of paper. Because of controlled indoor climate, factories did not have to shut down because of extreme heat. Products could be made and workers could stay on the job. This invention revolutionized industry worldwide. In 1906, a creamery was air cooled; 1926 home air conditioning became available; in 1949 skyscrapers were air conditioned; and in 1952 malls were air conditioned. Although Carrier died in 1950, his company continued to progress in commercial air conditioning. The invention revolutionized the way we live. Auto air conditioning was formerly a luxury but today is "standard."

God has put inventions, knowledge, and skill in his people for the betterment of all. In this 2020 season, Sam Caster, a businessman, joined with a pharmaceutical company that captured the essence of the aloe vera plant to restore the human immune system to fight of disease naturally. He has freely distributed the product to children dying of disease in poor countries. There has been a great turn around in child mortality in these places.

God has an inheritance for you rich in mercy and grace. He will provide everything you will ever need at the right time, but you need to prepare before God will release all. As a doctor, you cannot receive the fullness of the profession until you have studied, passed the exams, done grueling intern work, and have proven that you are capable of the responsibility. The purpose of success is to give God glory. He will give you supernatural abilities and opportunities because He wants to say to you, "Well done! Good and faithful servant." (Matthew 25:21)

God's plan for you is for good and not for evil. Do not disdain your time in history. Do not disdain your lineage. Your ancestors suffered through hardships so that you could reap the benefits. Honor them. Do not disdain your gifts and talents. Acknowledge them. Thank the Lord you have them. Don't waste your time comparing yourself to others and their destiny with jealousy or envy.

I am grateful that I am living at this time in history. God is doing great things around the globe. He has His hand on all mankind bringing them into His Kingdom.

The Call

You may have an exalted idea that a "call" is something esoteric, or magical. I have been a teacher, wife, mother, Girl Scout leader, Cub Scout leader, hostess, office worker, homemaker, Sunday school teacher, and a prayer warrior. All of those served God's purpose. Though not all at once, I believe I have been *called* to all those roles. I am sure I have affected many lives positively along the way. God may have put you in someone's path to be their greatest encourager or the one that turns their life around. Look at yourself and see what you have been doing and what you can do. Find the fruit that you are bearing. As long as you are alive, you are called to influence somebody for the kingdom of God.

I received a thank-you note from a young high school graduate who worked as a temporary employee at the office where I was the department supervisor. She told me that she had expected to do simple flunky jobs to earn some money and bide her time before going to college. By the end of the summer, she realized that she learned much more than she would have in a classroom. She had learned integrity on the job, about getting along with co-workers, and telephone skills. Because I incorporated her into the workplace she had the best possible experience. I knew this was just a summer job, but did not diminish her importance to the team. I maximized the job experience that will stay with her throughout her life.

God wants to have a personal relationship with you. He wants to partner with you in answering your prayers and the prayers of others. He is neither a Santa Claus nor an angry Judge. He is not Santa Claus dispensing gifts based on your good behavior. He won't give you something beyond your capability no matter how much you want it. A 10-year-old boy may want a car, but his father is going to make him wait until he can drive legally and responsibly.

Everyone will stand in before Him for judgment based on obedience. He is a merciful Judge not because he will look the other way and let you off the hook but because he has provided a Savior, Jesus Christ. You are not sinless but you can be blameless. Only Jesus was sinless. We become blameless when we repent and forgive. Salvation through Jesus Christ allows you to repent and forgive (as we did in the foregoing chapters) so that wrath of judgment does not come on you. If you try to know God the Father without knowing the Son Jesus, you will miss the grace of salvation. If you refuse to believe in the Son, you stand in God's wrath instead of His mercy.

Leave Mistakes Behind

Three Realms

Three realms are operating simultaneously in the supernatural.

The first realm is here on earth where daily life happens. You awaken, you go to work, and you care for your family. All your physical senses are engaged in this first realm.

The second realm is where the devil (the Prince of the Air) operates. The devil wants to keep you from your destiny because when you fulfill that destiny to any degree, God will be glorified. The devil hates anything God loves, including you. Demonic activity operates invisibly in the second realm and the earthly realm to capture you with negative influence, deception, blindness, and even direct attack. These powers lure you into sin by thought, word, and deed.

Sin is the devil's trap! The devil lies to you whispering with your voice to get you to agree with him. You think it is your own thought. When a traumatic event happens you will hear "It's all your fault," "God doesn't care about you or he would have stopped it," or "Now you will be scarred for life and you can't do anything about it." He will plant fear saying, "Watch out, it will happen again if you are not careful." He will then somehow make sure that a similar thing does happen. All those thoughts isolate you from God. If the devil cannot get you to believe his whispered lies, he will use those around you to speak his lies. They will betray you, reject you, and criticize you without even knowing they are doing the devil's dirty work. The devil will give you proof that his lies are true with news stories, movies, and even comic strips. He will minimize good things or disguise the blessings of God by saying it was by luck, chance, or coincidence. He will use every means to discredit God including your judgmental thoughts and careless words. You do not have to accept these lies. Your conscience is your heavenly plumb line.

Trying to do the will of God by your human strength is futile. God never intended for you to do it on your own. He sent Jesus and the Holy Spirit to help you be successful. Repentance and forgiveness pierce the dark blockade of the second realm. Jesus came to be your Savior removing the chains of sin. Only through repentance and forgiveness can the chains of sin be supernaturally broken. You cannot work them off, or ignore them, or hope time will make them disappear. Repent for the things you have chosen that were out of alignment with God, and forgive those who pushed you off track with God's. This will set you free to ascend to the third realm. This is the reason you have been led through the many exercises of repentance and forgiveness.

God is on His throne waiting for you. The heavenly hosts dwell with Him in the third realm waiting for his orders to

Leave Mistakes Behind

assist you. After having sin removed, you can ascend through worship to the third realm to get strategy, strength, and the power to bring heaven to earth. Bringing the Kingdom from heaven to earth is your assignment and privilege because when you do, you are victoriously fulfilling your destiny.

When Jesus is your Savior and Commander-in-Chief, the devil has no way of stopping you. You have the backing of the heavenly host. When you heed the commands from the throne room, you are empowered to descend to earth to carry out His will. Supernatural help will come in the form of assistance or empowerment. When you have a task, such as passing an exam or leading a group, ask for empowerment. The Holy Spirit will enable you to carry out the task successfully. When you have an assignment to wage war against evil or to protect territory, ask for heavenly reinforcements to assist you.

Your Alert System

Standard issue in the military includes a uniform, a military ID, and weapons. The Christian receives a garment of righteousness, an ID as a child of God, and the indwelling of the Holy Spirit. Today, praying in the Holy Spirit is a standard issued weapon for the soldiers of God. Think of this vocal gift of praying in the power of the Holy Spirit as your cell phone to God. Cell phones allow you to make calls, receive calls, get information, get directions, send texts, take pictures, record memos, make videos, and share information. When you use the gift of praying in the Spirit, you can do all the above with heaven at any time simultaneously. You can access it while driving (no law against praying while driving), showering, on a coffee break, and in private devotions. This does not make you better than others, just better equipped.

My Story

At the time I was struggling with depression, I could not pray or be spiritual in any way. A prayer minister prayed with me for inner healing, then told me I had to strengthen my "spirit man." (Jude 1:20) She could only pray for me on the outside, but I had to do something on the inside to break out of the trap of depression. She

Leave Mistakes Behind

suggested I receive the baptism of the Holy Spirit and start praying in tongues. She was a godly woman with much inner strength so I took her advice. She prayed for me to receive the baptism of the Holy Spirit and told me to practice praying in an unknown language. In the beginning, that amounted to making vocal sounds I didn't understand but submitted them to the Holy Spirit to make sense out of it. First I started with various forms of "alleluia" repeated quickly. That morphed into gibberish. I practiced whenever I had a chance in the car, in the shower, or just daydreaming. Like practicing scales on the piano, it eventually became easy and fluid. The most difficult part was trying to *not* understand what I was praying. Whenever my brain got in the way, I would return to gibberish on purpose. Whenever I was with people who prayed in tongues, I would join in whether or not I knew what I was doing. Yielding the mind and the tongue to the Holy Spirit takes you to another level of spiritual freedom. As the Bible says, when we do not know how to pray, let the Holy Spirit pray through you. (Romans 8:26-27) This requires a mix of trust and faith. Through the years, I have developed the gift of tongues with several languages. Although I cannot identify the languages, the Holy Spirit chooses the appropriate one each time.

On one occasion, I volunteered as a scribe to help missionary doctors in Mexico. As the day was ending, there was still a long line of people waiting to enter the clinic. We only had an hour left before flying out in daylight.

"Let me pray for these people waiting in line." I offered.

"You do healing prayer? Yeah, let's go for it!" The director told the people the clinic was closing but if they wanted prayer, they could get in line for prayer. The adults with many children formed a separate line in front of me.

I was new at praying in the spirit but I jumped in because I only spoke English and they spoke only Spanish. I have seen other ministers pray in the spirit so I started. The adults were wary so they sent their children first. I held the child's hands, smiled, and prayed in the spirit. Each I touched started to giggle and laugh such happy laughs. I'm guessing the parents asked them why they were laughing but they just laughed and it spread from child to child. Finally, some adults approached me for prayer.

"asdf asd asd asdf asdf, " I prayed in tongues as I held their hands. They smiled and answered me in Spanish. I didn't know what they said, but I just answered in tongues. They would nod and move away for the next person. I do not know what I prayed but by their demeanor, I gathered it was something good. Some had smiles, others had tears. This was supernatural!

Acts 2:6 says that they "heard" their native tongues. I believe this is what was happening. The people I prayed for heard it in Spanish even though I was praying in tongues. As we prepared to leave and I was no longer in prayer mode, two ladies came up to me speaking in Spanish. They were so puzzled when I told them I didn't speak Spanish.

God can still converse with you in your limited earthly language, but praying in tongues boosts your prayer life exponentially. It frees you from having to translate and think in an earthly language. Heaven's language is infinite. This Holy Spirit cell phone is free when you ask for it. (Luke 11:13) You just have to learn how to use it.

Prayer:

"Father you said you will give me the Holy Spirit when I ask. I am asking for a "Holy Spirit cell phone" so that I can communicate with you in a heavenly language. Thank you for the gift that leads me to pray."

Begin praying in an unknown language starting with unintelligible sounds or various forms of "alleluia." Try saying "toy boat" very fast and accept whatever comes out. This can be fun as well as funny. For some, the new language happens instantly. For me, it took practice. Just as a young child builds vocabulary over time, babble turns into language, and your spiritual vocabulary expands with usage. Join with someone who already prays in tongues. It's like playing tennis with someone better than you to build your skill. If you already pray in the spirit, be charged up 100% ready to go.

Chapter 6
Preparing for Your Future

You can make three important preparations for receiving answered prayers. (1) Build a suitable habitation for the Holy Spirit. (2) Be a holy vessel. (3) Adopt a quality lifestyle.

A Suitable Habitation

Build your life intentionally with the finest materials available to you so you will be a place suitable for a holy God to dwell. The Three Little Pigs built their houses of straw, sticks, and bricks. Their houses were supposed to protect them from the Big Bad Wolf who would blow down their houses and make them his prey. The devil will blow on your life seeking to make you his prey.

Laziness, broken promises, and carelessness are like straw put together based on convenience. Every situation becomes an emergency in the storms of life. If you are not destroyed, you will need to be rescued.

The materials of a house of sticks may be better, but they are self-centered and non-sacrificial. When the storms of life come, the house cannot withstand the force of the wind and it will be blown down. Also in this case, you will need to be rescued.

In contrast, sacrifice, excellence, and high integrity are materials of a house of bricks that will withstand hurricanes in life. Unexpected events cannot destroy you. You will stand on solid ground and you will be able to rescue others.

You can be sure that life will present you with many opportunities to build character. God's plan for your life requires a character that reflects Him. You do not awaken one morning and suddenly have a good character. Perseverance is built on many failures and successes. Integrity is only built after many commitments are met. (Romans 5:3-5)

A Worthy Vessel

God is always pouring out blessings. You will want to be a vessel aligned with God in *position* under the blessing spout. However, you must be in a *condition* to retain the blessings. If you are holding on to bad attitudes and judgment, you will be like a sieve that drains the blessings away. A vessel soiled with unconfessed sin and unforgiveness will contaminate the blessings. The best vessel is a large one that has been cleansed by repentance and forgiveness. It can be filled to overflowing with plenty to share with others.

Meditate on what kind of vessel you are. If you are a small vessel, ask the Holy Spirit to expand you. If you are full of holes, patch them by changing your attitude. If you are soiled, repent and forgive to be washed clean. Get ready to benefit from the blessings poured into you.

Quality Lifestyle

Chaos is not God's style.

God ordered the stars and planets in their courses. He ordered the laws of nature and the spiritual laws of mankind. God wants you to have order in your life, not rigidity. Just as the right vessel is necessary to receive the blessings, the right lifestyle is necessary to manifest the blessings. God wants to show off His glory through you.

Intentionally put *rest, exercise, and a healthy diet* in your life. Your body is not a machine that can go non-stop without bad consequences. Sleep deprivation will rob you of an alert mind, clear thinking, and physical energy. Incorporate some kind of intentional exercise in your life. If just waving your arms is the best you can do, do it. My friend Pat is recovering from a stroke that paralyzed her left side. The physical therapist advised her to move her arm as much as possible. When I visit her, she waves her arm and rotates her wrist all the time we are talking. Take the stairs, work out in a gym or public park, and join active athletics. Listen to your body and stay away from foods that adversely affect you.

A Story

When my mother was 85 years old, she was diagnosed with diabetes. She did all the daily testing, took pills, and tried to control her diet her way. She was resigned to managing diabetes with medications for the rest of her life. At age 89, she moved to assisted living where her medications and diet were regulated with no short cuts. Within months her diabetes went away and she lived her last years to age 93 diabetes-free. Another elderly friend had the same problem with the same possible solution. However, while his assisted living place provided the proper diabetic regimen, he refused to eat what was provided. He soon died of a diabetic coma at the age of 87. God uses health professionals to help you. These are all part of physical well- being to give glory to God. You are

Preparing for Your Future

more valuable to God when you are alive than when you are dead.

Work, study, and recreation are mainstays of keeping an active mind. *Work* keeps you alert, active, and engaged. Volunteer if you do not have a paid job or are retired. *Study* something— sports, history, mathematics, chess, etc.—to keep your mind engaged. Exercise all your faculties to be a well-tuned instrument. For *recreation*, hang out with friends, play sports, join book clubs, or take up hobbies, like kite flying. Our bodies, minds, and souls need a well-balanced life.

Habitation

Your *living space and time* affect you more than you may realize. Make your living space clean, livable, and organized. Always searching for things steals your time. *Time* cannot be replaced. Frequently having to replace items you could not find drains your pocketbook. Set priorities, budget your time, and step out of chaos so you will be productive.

A healthy *spiritual life* should not be left to chance. Participate in regular faith functions such as worship, prayer meetings, and study groups. Keep a personal devotional time. Seek spiritual direction from a wise counselor or mentor. Your spiritual life should be ongoing, not just for emergencies.

Financial Order

If you have in the past mismanaged your money by writing bad checks, not repaying a loan, or cheated someone financially, repent and forgive. Saying, "I don't do that anymore," does not remove the consequences past financial sin. A financial order is about faithfulness and stewardship, not money. If you are in lack, there is a remedy.

Preparing for Your Future

A young man came to me for prayer. He explained, "We want to move to a better place. Our current apartment is cramped. The neighbors unfriendly and just don't feel good there. We can't move because our FICO scores are low and the credit checks disqualify us."

"Tell me about your money management," I asked. "Do you have a savings account?"

"No. We barely have enough to pay the bills." "What is your biggest debt?"

"I have a student loan of $30,000. I graduated five years ago." "How much have you paid back?"

"Nothing. We just don't have the money."

"Give up your Starbucks. Buy groceries at a cheaper store. Pay something on your student loan no matter how small. If you get any cash for birthday or Christmas gifts, use them to pay back the student loan. Then watch the Lord work on your behalf. Prove yourself responsible for the loan that gave you the gift of a college education."

Nine months later he reported, "I did what you said. My wife got a salary raise, and I got more cash gifts than ever to put toward the loan. I found 90% off sales, and make coffee at home. My credit score went up enough to be accepted for a better apartment."

He learned to steward his money in practical ways rather than moan about what he did not have.

Another woman told me, "I am tired of depending on church pantries for food. My part-time income was just not enough."

"Tell me about your spending habits," I asked.

"I use my credit card so I don't have to carry around cash."

"Do you spend only what you have in cash so you can pay off the credit card in the first month?"

"No. I pay the minimum."

"So the balance keeps growing? If you only pay the minimum, how much of it is late-fees or interest?"

"I don't know."

After sharing with me her spending habits, I discovered she was depending on a credit card and getting deeper in debt. Because she was not paying all her bills on time, she was using almost half her income on late fees. A little change in habit to pay on time would double her income. Also, she was buying expensive cosmetics which she could not afford. Perhaps in the future, when she had commensurate wealth she could consider such an expensive luxury. It was a want and not a need. God could then work on her behalf when she learned to steward properly.

Separate your needs from your wants. Pay your bills on time. Save for emergencies. Tithe to your church community. Create future investment opportunities. God gives you the *power* to get wealth so you need to use that power acting responsibly with what you have at your disposal so He can increase you. (Deuteronomy 8:17-20)

Emotional Order

Emotional order will prevent an emotional whirlwind of sin. Anger is a combination of emotions that include resentment, frustration, hate, and bitterness. Unchecked anger draws you into sin against others and yourself. Grumbling kept the Israelites from entering the Promised Land. (Psalm 106:25-27) Moses forfeited his chance to enter the Promised Land because of anger. (Psalm 106:32) If you constantly fill the atmosphere with gossip, backbiting, or criticisms, you will always be emotionally agitated. Control your tongue. Know when to be quiet. Do not get involved in an argument for the sake of arguing. (Matthew 12:26)

Healthy Relationships

Debbie complained, "Why do people always push me around and talk mean to me?"

"Do you talk to others the same way?" I asked "Yes, because they do it to me!"

"Do you realize you are stirring up behaviors you don't like?"

After repenting of retaliating, I suggested she learn how to be respectful rather than retaliate. The anger in her heart stopped her from being calm.

"I get so irritated and hurt when people ask about my private life and give me unwanted advice."

"Try responding with this: 'It's a private matter' or 'I plan to decide for myself.'"

With a short lesson and a few tips on respectful phrases, she agreed to try a new way of responding. There is no need to make a scene or to become agitated. That need to retaliate was keeping her trapped.

Keep *boundaries* and *respect*. Know your boundaries by respecting yourself. Express yourself with respectful words. Don't use scowling, eye-rolling, or smirking. Smile!!! Respect other people's boundaries regardless if you don't agree with them. Refrain from demeaning, criticizing, or judging. Many people didn't like Jesus, but he did not demean or disrespect them.

Intentionally build good relationships. They do not happen magically. They are developed and nurtured. Do not assume everyone who enters your life is good for you. You must discern who is for you and who is against you.

Comfort and encourage others. Acknowledge feelings or situations even if you don't agree on everything. Phrases like "That sounds frustrating," "Oh, how frightening that must have been," or even an "Oh, no!" can be comforting. The silent treatment and the cold shoulder are relationship breakers. During a lunch break at a conference, I joined a woman who was also alone. We struck up a conversation and discovered we had much in common so we were able to encourage each other throughout the conference.

Financial integrity, emotional stability, and order in relationships with others brings glory to God. There must be a balance between the spiritual and the natural earthly life. Although you are responsible for these areas of your life, you don't have to do it all alone. The Holy Spirit is your supernatural Helper when you move to have a lifestyle congruent with God. If you are faithful in little, you will be faithful in much. (Luke 16:10) Pay attention to the "little" so that the "much" can flow in.

After reading the above paragraphs, you may think of other areas of your life that need order. List the ones you want to reorder in your life.

_____

_____

_____

Prayer

"Lord I desire to have order in my life in the areas of (list as many as you want).

I repent for what I have done and not done that allow chaos in those areas. (List any specific actions or inactions that come to mind .)

I forgive myself for opening the door to chaos. Give me a new beginning with wisdom on how to put order into my life so I can reflect you. Send me people who will help me. Send me situations that will establish me in your ways. Open my eyes and ears to be sensitive to your leading. Thank you, Lord, for supernatural help. Amen

The Church Home

The Church of the 21st century is not like the church your grandparents or maybe even your parents attended. The Church has grown up. If you are a new Christian or if you

Preparing for Your Future

have drifted from the Church through the years, connect with a church family who will walk with you. Every Christian needs community while walking in righteousness and daily communion with the Lord. I am referring to the worldwide gathering of those who follow Jesus. The internet, live streaming, television, and air travel have made the Church global. It is not confined to the immediate neighborhood anymore. Yes, there are many flavors but we are still one Church. It's important to find a "flavor" that gives you spiritual support. A "Lone Ranger Christian" is a set up for an ambush. "Where no counsel is, the people fall: but in the multitude of counselors there is safety." (Proverbs 11:14 KJV)

Jesus said, "I will build my Church" (Mathew 16:18) and yet we have made all kinds of plans and programs of what we thought the Church should be. God's plan is laid out in the book of the Acts of the Apostles and the letters in the New Testament. He knew we needed the five gifts of Apostles, Prophets, Evangelists, Pastors, and Teachers to equip the people for ministry. (Ephesians 4:11) We need all five to equip us to fulfill our destiny. It has taken the church decades to learn to walk in those ministries but it is here now.

Jesus demonstrated all five functions during his earthly life. As the *Evangelist*, He said, "Follow Me," and people did. Jesus the *Pastor* healed the sick and cast out demons.

Jesus the *Teacher* taught them the Scriptures and what the Kingdom of God was like. Jesus the *Prophet* announced what the Father was saying and doing. He was totally in sync with God's plan of salvation. Jesus the *Apostle* sent his followers out by twos to preach, heal, and deliver. Finally, before he left the earthly realm, He sent out his twelve apostles commissioning them to carry out the work of the Kingdom until He comes again.

Evangelists have the anointing to draw people to Christ through their testimony and their preaching. They usually have charisma and enthusiastic zeal for life with Christ that attracts the searching heart. The Evangelists need to connect his newly won souls to a *Pastor* who gives comfort, binds up wounds, and guides people through the healing and deliverance processes. A new Christian, with new strength, needs to be connected to the *Teacher* who will show the ways of godly living and ways of applying God's principles. Teachers encourage and admonish to help members grow in strength and knowledge of the Lord, and stay out of the devil's traps. Teachers can be found online, at conferences, in Bible classes, and through personal mentoring.

Although all have the gift of prophecy, the office of Prophet is a leader appointed by God and confirmed by the Church. *Prophets* carry the authority of God, not just information. Prophets declare the Kingdom building vision and encourage the Church along the way, both corporately and individually.

Finally, *Apostles* bring order in the Church by giving direction for how the tasks will be done. The Prophets and Apostles must work together because they both hear from God for different reasons. The Prophets declare what God is declaring, and Apostles set things in motion and send the people out to do what the Prophet declared.

Ideally, each church congregation should have all five ministries operating as a team. Today, Apostolic Centers are springing up all over the world operating with developed five- fold ministries. Fortunately, in the age of the internet, quick travel, and multimedia you can have is access to all five-fold ministries for spiritual growth. The Lord will orchestrate those ministries for you if you do not have access to the five-fold ministries at your home church. This book is written especially for those who do not have access to pastoral/teaching.

It is still important to be connected with a home church or group where you can interact personally. You need a group who knows you, who will pray for you, and be with you to share your ups and downs. Jesus had Peter, James, and John. You too need an inner circle.

Ask the Lord who are the five-fold ministers in your life. If any is lacking, ask the Lord to connect you.

1. Evangelist = Someone who reminds you who is Lord of your life
2. Pastor = Someone who gives comfort, healing, and deliverance
3. Teacher = Someone who teaches you how to walk with Jesus
4. Prophet = Someone who gives vision and speaks encouragement to you
5. Apostle = Someone who supports and guides you when you step out in the new territory

Chapter 7
Come Celebrate

God gave Moses the model of the Tabernacle to be the place for God's presence. That model is a visual and experiential pattern that even today is relevant for us to follow to enter into worship. Jesus said He was the tabernacle so it's important to know the tabernacle set up and what it tells us meeting God today.

The Israelites had lived for 400 years under pagan gods and rituals, so when they left Egypt for the Promised Land, they had to learn to worship a mighty, unseen God. He said his name is "I AM." They were accustomed to seeing idols so this was a new experience for them in the wilderness. Even when they tried to keep worshipping "I AM", traditions got mixed up and they reverted to the golden calf.

God gave Moses exact measurements, exact materials, and the exact protocol for the Tent of the Presence. He wanted the people to know His *presence,* not his image. He is greater than any image. No image could capture "I AM."

God was reinstating obedience so He gave prescribed ways of worship. He was not being legalistic. He had a long-range plan for the salvation of mankind that required obedience. "Then have them make a *sanctuary* for me, and I will dwell among them. Make this tabernacle and all its furnishings exactly like the pattern I will show you." (Exodus 27:8-9) You can turn on a lamp to enjoy the light before you understand how it works. Obedience comes first. Understanding follows.

I am giving only an abbreviated description of the Tabernacle of the Presence, and not a historical study, because the purpose here is to relate a pattern for you to approach worship. There is a protocol in worship through which you can benefit the most because it sets your mind and heart in order--ready to hear, see, and experience God. Remember, preparation is not for God to hear you. Preparation is for *you* to hear God.

To come into His presence was a sacred rite. The first place to pause was at the laver to wash hands, feet, and head to remove all unclean elements of life. The second pause was at the altar of sacrifice where shed blood represented redemption from sin. Grains and produce were also brought as offerings.

People waited in the outer court while the priests entered the Inner Court. Priests were assigned as representatives to represent the people before God. These were men who observed purification rituals. Behind the separating curtain were three stations in the Inner Court—(1) the Lampstand of pure gold representing the Word of God burning 24/7, (2) the table with the Bread of the Presence representing God's provision for all times, and the (3) Table of Incense, signifying prayers offered 24/7. Beyond the Inner Court, was the Holy of Holies wherein rested the Ark of the Covenant that they carried through the wilderness into the Promised Land. Aaron's budded rod of authority and appointment, an omer of mana of provision, and the tablets of the Ten Commandments of God's laws were housed in the Ark. Only once a year the high priest was allowed to enter the Holy of Holies after being ritually cleansed, and making a sacrifice offered on behalf of the whole community. The Holy of Holies was separated from the rest of the Temple by a very thick curtain, like a portable wall, reported to be six inches thick of combined materials woven together. This curtain protected the people from being decimated by the holiness of God. This is the curtain that was torn in two when Jesus died on the cross. Jesus was the pure Lamb of God, sacrificed for the people. At the time of Jesus' death, the curtain was supernaturally torn in two signifying Jesus made it now possible for mankind to have a face to face relationship with God.

Begin to Dance

First, survey your life situation to see if anything is out of line with God's Word and His will. Consider the areas pointed out in this book. As in the tabernacle, approach the laver first as a place of repentance and forgiveness. Repent of any known sin or any sin that the Holy Spirit reveals to you. Forgive anyone or anything that has sinned against you. Wash away the ties of sin that hamper you.

Secondly, come to the altar of sacrifice. Be ready to lay down something personal that blocks God from any part of your life—old habits, idols you have created, or lusts of the flesh. Since Jesus was the ultimate sacrifice for your sin, you can lay it down on the altar in repentance and forgiveness the same way you have in the earlier chapters of this book. Let go of any behaviors, thinking, and emotional ties that do not glorify God.

Thirdly, prepare your offering of praise, thanksgiving, and wealth. Thank Him for the sun rising on you another day, for a new job, or a call from an estranged child. Praise him that he never leaves you or forsakes you. Make your wealth offering a representation of your praise. If you have no money, ask the Lord to put something in your hand that you can give. It may be a flower or a note you have written that says, "I love you, Lord."

Fourthly, bring your prayer requests for yourself, your loved ones, and the world. Praying for yourself is not selfish. You know what you need and want. Humility is activated when we humbly ask according to His Word. God is looking to fulfill His Word, not your bright ideas.

Begin The Worship Festivities

1. Come Rejoicing

Once you have prepared, come rejoicing into the Outer Court. Use the same enthusiasm you would have when entering the stadium for your favorite sports game. Enter his gates with thanksgiving and into his courts with praise. Sing and exalt God.

2. Proceed to the laver

"I repent of my sin known or unknown, things done and left undone, especially…(losing my cool with my husband, holding anger against my boss, starting my day without checking in with God first, putting myself down, etc.).

I forgive those who have sinned against me in any way, intentionally or unintentionally. I release them from any debt to me—no restitution, no apology, no reasons, no explanations, and no excuses needed. I receive by faith, the forgiveness of sin through Jesus. By faith, I accept that I am cleansed of my sin. Amen."

3. Altar of Sacrifice

"I choose to lay down *my self-accusing thoughts and behaviors*. I repent of agreeing with the devil rather than God. I forgive myself for sinning against me and I release myself 100%. I choose to lay down *my gossiping about others and passing judgments. I repent of hurtful words and harsh judgments against others.* I forgive those who have judged me and I release them 100%. They owe me no restitution, no apology, no reasons, no explanations, and no excuses.

4. Enter the Inner Court at the Lampstand

"I invite the light of Christ to shine on me and illuminate his Word in my heart. I accept the revelations of the Holy Spirit for my life."

5. Table of the Bread of the Presence (Communion Table)

"I receive Jesus as the Bread of My Life. I declare that he is my sustenance and provides all that I need."

"I receive the Blood of Jesus for the forgiveness of sins." (If available, take Communion in the presence of God.)

6. Altar of Incense

Submit your prayer requests according to His Word. (examples)

a. Lord, you are the Healer. I ask for *healing for my body, my mother, my boss.*
b. You are the Provider. *Provide my son's college tuition.*
c. You are the Prince of Peace: *Bring peace into my household.*
d. You are the Good Shepherd: *Comfort Sally in her time of mourning.*
e. Nothing is impossible for you*: Move the hearts of our state leaders to righteousness.*

7. Enter the Holy of Holies.

Remember that when Jesus died on the cross the curtain of the temple was torn in two, making it possible for you to come with confidence to the throne of grace. (Hebrews 4:16)

All scriptures are from NIV. This is the time to lift the name of Jesus and be focused on his face and not his hand. Sing of your love for Him. Tell Him how grateful you are for what He is doing in your life. Pray and sing in the Holy Spirit. After lifting your voice, spend time in silence listening to Him tell you what's on *His* heart. He may speak to you in visions, audible voice, inner voice, emotions, and even through someone else. Do not limit God. Be patient! His sheep hear His voice.

8. Worship Everyday

The supernatural nature of worship flows into your daily life making it supernatural. This tabernacle pattern is effective for personal worship and corporate worship. In addition, Bible study or preaching is enriched by worship.

Amen and Amen

When your heart, mind, and lifestyle are right with God, you will have no fear of coming to the throne boldly. There is such a wealth of richness, power, and intimacy behind the door of heaven. The door will open when you are ready to partake of its riches. The door will open to you as the promises of God are for now. The ten wise maidens were prepared for the bridegroom's coming. The unwise maidens were caught unprepared. This book is to help you be prepared to enter into the richness of God's supernatural presence which is available to you every day. You are now prepared to dance with the Lord!

Index

Chapter 2: Video teaching

https://bethanyprojects.org/teaching-videos/wholeness-joy-and-freedom.

Chapter3: For video teaching on this topic, go to

https://bethanyprojects.org/teaching-videos/generational-freedom.

Chapter 4: "Breaking the Bondages of Sin"

workshop video is available for viewing at http://www.bethanyprojects.org/Closing-Doors-of-Sin.

Chapter 5: Leave Mistakes Behind

https://bethanyprojects.org/videos/freedom-from-yesterday-s-mistakes

Chapter 6: Preparing for Your Future

https://bethanyprojects.org/teaching-videos/the-cry-that-god-hears.

Chapter 7: Worship

https://bethanyprojects.org/teaching-videos/the-cry-that-god-hears.

This ministry is under the umbrella of Hidden With Christ Ministries. You may support Marcia Chang Vogl's ministry online.
Hiddenwithchrist.org.
Select: http://www.bethanyprojects.org.

―――――

Bethany Projects reaches out to women who compose a very large and important part of the Church and society:

Women who are often overlooked in the Church are 1) Single women who have never married, 2) Divorced women, 3) Widows, and 4)those whose husbands do not share the same spiritual walk as they do.

Ministry to them includes:

1. Praying for/with them individually
2. Spiritual counseling
3. Healing
4. Setting them free from their past.
5. Deliverance from demonic influences
6. Providing Godly fellowship

7. Encouragement
8. Establishing a Biblical mindset
9. Training them to walk with the Holy Spirit
10. Mentoring to minister, to pray, to worship, and engage in spiritual warfare

Life experiences Marcia can share on God's interactions include:

1. Marriage covenant partnership (53 years)
2. Career Woman (public school music teacher, mortgage industry)
3. Manage a household
4. Child care and rearing, child bearing, adoption
5. Full time mom of three children
6. Working mom earning money for children's college
7. Finances: manage daily budget, investments, giving, planning
8. Sickness: care for self and family
9. Family events, parents, in-laws, reunions, relatives
10. Student: earn college degrees and ministry degrees
11. Minister: balance ministry & family,
12. Travel internationally for leisure and work.

Ministry is offered through:

1. Published books: *The Path Forward, Dancing With God, Training to Reigh With God*
2. Blogs and devotionals
3. Videos and audio recordings
4. Private sessions: in person, online
5. Group prayer meetings
6. Teaching Biblical principles
7. Group ministry
8. Retreats
9. Workshops
10. Mentoring groups
11. Social Media: Facebook, Instagram, Linkedn, website.

The Biblical principles taught apply to men and women, young and old. All are welcomed to learn and participate.

To request an invitation submit your email to info@marciavhangvogl.com to receive the Skype link and the prepared lesson.

Online or in-person ministry is provided on a donation basis.

Donations to support the ministry are accepted online at https://hiddenwithchrist.org/donate-to-bethany-projects.

More information about Bethany Projects can be found at

www.marciachangvogl.com

———

Contact Marcia Chang Vogl

info@marciavhangvogl.com
https://www.facebook.com/bethanyprojects/
Instagram/Marcia.prayer
Email: Marcia.prayer@gmail.com
Dancingwithgodbook.com

Also by Marcia Chang Vogl

The Path Forward

Dancing With God:

The Christian Journey to Live Supernaturally

Training to Reign With God:

The Christian Guide to Spiritual Maturity

———

Contact Marcia Vogl

marciachangvogl.com

info@marciavhangvogl.com

www.ingramcontent.com/pod-product-compliance
Lightning Source LLC
Chambersburg PA
CBHW052140070526
44585CB00017B/1905